Chasing The Crown

An Unauthorized History of Boxing's Richest Prize

Anton Shapiro

authorHOUSE®

AuthorHouse™ UK Ltd.
500 Avebury Boulevard
Central Milton Keynes, MK9 2BE
www.authorhouse.co.uk
Phone: 08001974150

First published by AuthorHouse   11/15/2010

ISBN: 978-1-4520-2957-3 (sc)

This book is printed on acid-free paper.

To my daughters Min and Devorah
and my grandson Oliver

Forward

The word purity has a strictness about it, but when it comes to the fight game, it simply defines those who really care about the sport. At one time it was called the Noble Art and the Sweet Science. Few would refer to it any longer in those terms. The respect has gone. There are still die hard fight fans to be sure. But in general sports lovers have deserted the game in droves. There are still mega bucks to be made, but largely it has degenerated into a fringe sport. The time when Marciano's title defences were headline news is long gone and unlikely to return. Moreover, the dignity of the word champion is lost. A champion is simply that. Now we have three or more champions at the same weight. This is not to be credited or taken seriously. A champion can now be stripped of a hard won title by the stroke of a pen by some overfed bureaucrat who would find it hard to run for a bus. But like it or not, that is the reality of boxing. One can add to this by mentioning many current 'historians', who twist the facts of the game and malign some of the great names of the sport in the name of some twisted concept of 'political correctness'. For what it is worth, racialism in boxing, or anywhere else for that matter, belongs in the slop bucket. But frankly, so do much of the writings of these half baked 'historians'. The hardest response they get is to make one wince at their diabolical ignorance Here we are hoping to give a fairer and more balanced view, as opposed to the bias and shallow fact twisting that is setting in today.

Tom vs. Tom

One of the earliest victims of this current political revisionism is the old bare knuckle bruiser, Tom Cribb. It might seem unfair to have some sympathy for Cribb, as he was allegedly, the beneficiary of an unfair act. There is some evidence that he was not. Yet there have been attempts to soil his reputation to the point of stupidity. In Cribb's climb to the top he had built up a formidable reputation. He had defeated the great Jem Belcher twice, and then knocked out the ageless Bill Richmond after 50 hard fought rounds. The controversy started with Richmond's protégé, the powerful Tom Molineaux, a fellow Afro American. Molineaux found a backer with Richmond's aid, and battled his way up to challenge Cribb for the championship. The battle took place one cold December 18th 1810. There are different versions as to what actually happened. One is that Molineaux battered Cribb so badly; the champion was unable to come up to scratch within the allotted time. According to this version, and it is the one most generally accepted, Cribb's second, Joe Ward did some quick thinking. He accused the American of holding bullets in his fists in order to increase his punching power. A blazing row ensued. This gave Cribb time to recover, get his second wind, and then defeat Molineaux. Cribb, feeling he had bested the challenger fairly, retired from the game a national hero. The biggest uproar came about two hundred years later. Another version comes from a distinguished author, who went on national television to assure the viewers that Molineaux was the better fighter. Moreover he claimed, the crowd, in order to save Cribb and England's honour, ganged up on Molineaux, broke both his hands and six of his ribs. In that state, we are led to believe, he heroically battled on until Cribb stopped him in the 33rd round, or as some would have it the 39th. While some sympathy may be due to Molineaux, one would have to be a professional idiot to believe such a claim.

Finally, in keeping with the researches done for this book, the author obtained a copy of Pierce Eagan's authoritative 'Boxiana', primarily because it contained his round by round eye witness account of the fight. Here we have a somewhat different version, and this account is by no means unfair to Molineaux. In the 23rd round Cribb, as the other version stated, was at the end of his tether. Where it differs, is that Molineaux was almost in the same condition. The dilemma started when Molineaux, lacking the strength to finish Cribb off, pinned him against the ropes, and grabbed them with both hands. He held Cribb in such a way, that he could neither strike a blow nor fall down. The seconds of both fighters discussed ways of separating them.

TOM CRIBB

The umpires thought this could not be done until one of them fell down. At this point, the crowd became incensed. They rushed the outer ring and it is 'asserted that if one of Molineaux's fingers was not broken, it was much injured by some attempting to remove his hands from the ropes'. Meanwhile, Molineaux was gaining wind by burying his head on Cribb's chest, refusing to release his opponent. The crowd did not intervene because they thought Molinaux was winning, they tried to release his grip because they thought he was committing an unfair act. Cribb himself, by a desperate effort, broke free. Molineaux then got his head under his arm and 'fibbed away unmercifully' but he lacked the strength to finish him off. The wording now becomes ambiguous, it states...'the bets were now decided that Molineaux did not fight half an hour, that time expired during this round'. If a half hour respite was offered, Molineaux would have been just as grateful as Cribb. Although the official version states that the fight ended in the 33rd round, it was claimed that the 34th was the last round that might be called fighting. Eventually, Cribb emerged the stronger of the two. Molineaux went down and complained to his seconds that he could fight no more. They tried to persuade him to fight another round, but he fell from exhaustion and the fight ended in Cribb's favour.

The distinguished author went on to claim that Molineaux lost the rematch because he was demoralised, and had squandered his strength on loose women. His record implies something different. Cribb retired after the fight, feted, as stated, a national hero. Molineaux went on to defeat Joe Rimmer, and claimed the title. There was no hostile reaction from the crowd. There was a reaction from Cribb and his followers. They felt he must fight the American again to restore England's honour. Molineaux claimed after the rematch that he despaired of winning when he saw how physically fit Cribb looked. Cribb's benefactor, Captain Barclay had taken the fighter up to Scotland for nine weeks to increase his stamina and reduce his weight. He obviously thought Cribb was not as fit as he might have been in their first encounter. For all that Molineaux at first had the best of the milling. He closed Cribb's right eye, and seemed on the way to winning. Again, there was no hostile reaction from the crowd. Cribb then turned the fight around and broke the challenger's jaw. It was all over in 11 rounds.

There was undoubtedly a racial element in these fights, but they cannot be viewed in the same terms as today's political correctness. Very few English people would ever have seen a person of African origin. Cribb's loss would have been more a case of national pride than blatant racialism. The name Molineaux is French. Had he been a white Frenchman, the reaction of the crowd would have been far more hostile. The reason for this

TOM MOLINEAUX

being that these fights took place during the time of the Napoleonic wars. The French and English already had a long history of mutual antipathy. An Afro American could challenge Cribb for the championship on English soil. No French fighter at that time would have dared to have done so. If he had, then the six broken ribs and two broken hands would have been a far more realistic proposition.

It remains an open question as to whether Molineaux was robbed of victory, or he robbed himself by refusing to let go of the ropes, and thus antagonising the crowd. Moreover, their action does not seem to have been the deciding factor. Both men would have welcomed a long respite. Cribb recovered first as the stronger of the two.

In later times, other great fighters were given a reprieve one way or another. Harry Greb, Gene Tunney, Sugar Ray Robinson and Muhammad Ali were all offered this convenience, either by friendly referees, or fast thinking corner men. By and large their fans admired them enough to justify it, or better yet, to deny it ever happened.

The Noblest Roman of them all

The Boston Strong Boy

On rare occasions, a fighter of such stature will come along and dominate not only his era, but even overshadow the great names of those who come after him. Such a man was John Laurence Sullivan. John was the son of Irish immigrants. His mother was a big boned woman from County Roscommon. His father was a small, fiercely aggressive man from County Kerry. His grandfather had been a noted Celtic wrestler. His build was certainly inherited from his mother, his tireless aggression from his father. They had come to America, like thousands of other families, to escape the poverty and squalor that had driven the Irish to all parts of the English speaking world.

Yet in escaping to the 'Land of the Free', where the streets were supposedly paved with gold, most found they were not much better off from the hardship they had left behind them. Moreover, they were considered a troublesome minority group, largely uneducated, pugnacious and prone to drink. For most part they found it difficult to find decent work. People advertising for domestic help would usually require Americans, Swedish or Africans. The advert, more often than not, would finish with the phrase, 'No Irish need apply.' This phrase even became the name of a popular music hall song. Many Irish became slum dwellers, and Boston, Sullivan's home town, was the worst of all. The myth that America was the land of opportunity struck a bitter note for many Irish workers, including Sullivan's father. He was lucky enough to feed his family as a hod carrier. Twenty years later he was still a hod carrier. This may have been the reason he seemed to resent his son's success. When John won the title in 1882, his father's only response was, 'Champion of the world, is he? Why I could name a hundred men back in the Old Country that could have whipped him.'

Like many great American fighters, John could have made a career for himself as a professional baseball player. At first he took work with any employer that would have him. He might well have worked in a brewery, because he was said to have been able to lift a full beer barrel above his head. Later he would find a different use for the contents of the barrel. Gradually, like so many young Irishmen, he gravitated to the sport he was born for. His speed, boundless energy, and devastating punching power, marked him as an outstanding prize fighter right from the start. A powerful battler named Cocky Woods was said to have been the best fighter in Boston. That changed after he met Sullivan. This win gave John the right to go on an exhibition tour, culminating with him easily beating Dan Dwyer, the champion of Massachusetts. It was an exhibition bout with the world middle weight champion Mike Donavan that brought the youth to national attention. The youngster almost knocked him out. Joe Goss, a former claimant to the heavy weight title came next. John clearly outclassed him in a four round exhibition. There were no recognised ratings in those days, but John stopped some of the acknowledged contenders. A major breakthrough came when he met John Flood, known as the 'Bull's Head Terror'. John was now able to make some real money; the stake was a $1,000 dollars, with $750 going to the winner. The bout was held on a barge anchored in the river near Yonkers New York. The battle was slated to the finish with skin tight gloves under the Old London Prize Ring Rules. For all John Flood's formidable reputation, the finish came after only sixteen minutes. He was knocked down in every round, and wisely quit.

Sullivan then went on a knock out trail, taking on all comers. When John stopped Jack Burns in less than a round, negotiations were made for him to challenge Paddy

Paddy Ryan for the American, some said the world title. The fight was held in Mississippi City on February 7th 1882. It was a bare knuckle contest to the finish, and the finish came very quickly. Ryan went under in nine one sided rounds. Moreover, he attested to John's formidable punching power by stating that he felt as if a telegraph pole had been shoved against him sideways. For all that, he braved a well paid non title rematch. He was knocked cold inside three rounds. Some experts felt John's straightforward attack might have made him vulnerable to a scientific counter puncher. Yet Jem Mace, the greatest scientific fighter of his day and the father of the Australian fight school, asked John for an exhibition bout, providing the champion pulled his punches. Sullivan politely refused, stating he was unable to do that. The exhibition never came off. Looking at Sullivan's ten year tenure as champion, many have wondered, given his cantankerous nature and his desire for wealth, as to why he did not defend the title more often. The reason was simple enough. Prize fighting was an outlawed profession, and there were severe penalties to anyone caught practicing it. The trick of course, was not to get caught. Yet there were very few fighters who had not seen the inside of a prison cell, or paid a heavy fine. That included Sullivan himself. In most cases it was simply not worth it. To compensate for the risk and the financial damage, John went on tour, offering $1,000 to any man who could last four rounds with him. As these bouts were considered exhibitions, the law never bothered him. Moreover, as a sweetener, he assured all challengers that gloves would be worn.

Before the tour started he fought the English claimant to the heavyweight championship, Charley Mitchell. The fight was held at Madison Square Garden on May 4th 1883, under the new Marquis of Queensbury rules. The police were on hand, but seemingly just as observers. Mitchell was really a blown up middleweight who had taken the English heavyweight title. He was known as a scientific fighter with a stiff punch. John was made aware of this in the first round when Mitchell caught him with his feet too close together. He knocked him down. Observers said the champion was trying to claw his way back onto his feet before he even hit the canvas. There was no count. John leapt to his feet in a rage and chased Mitchell around the ring. He knocked him down but Charley covered up and hung on, out of breath but relatively unscathed. In the second round Mitchell hit the deck four times, then found himself sailing out of the ring and onto the floor. He barely made it back inside the ring with a badly damaged leg. In the third round John finally caught up with him. He battered him to the canvas. Charley was hurt, and the police stepped in to stop it for fear of a fatality. Charley gave them no arguments. No arrests were made.

Next came Jem Mace's protégé, the huge Maori Herbert A. Slade. This was another international contest. Sullivan ended his ambitions with a crunching right hand to the jaw in third round. Herbert did stay on as part of John's entourage on the tour. He finally quit, claiming there had to be more to life than being slapped around by John L. Sullivan every day. John however, was making more money with these exhibitions than he did in defending the title. Moreover in fifty of these fights, there was only one man, an Englishman, 'Tug Wilson', who picked up the prize money. He did so by running like a thief, and dropping to the canvas every time John came near him. It was claimed he went down 27 times in all. Sullivan claimed Wilson was down for 28 seconds at the first knock down. The Americans were so disgusted that English fighters thereafter had a hard time getting decent bouts. For all John's embarrassment, at least he did not have the police breathing down his neck.

Yet he knew, despite the risks, that he must defend the title at some point. He therefore agreed to accept Mitchell as a challenger. A year after their first fight, another had been arranged for June 30th 1884. This bout was cancelled as Sullivan was blind drunk and unable to stand on his feet. It was the first sign of John's addiction to drink. It was to seriously affect the rest of his professional career. When a title defence was arranged, the problem of a safe venue came up. Finally, the great philanthropist and business tycoon the Baron de Rothschild permitted his estate in Chantilly France, to be used as the battleground.

Mitchell was to admit after the fight, that he hoped John would have taken him too lightly, and not be in the best of physical condition. He planned to run and tire the 'Strong Boy' out, in the hope of eventually stopping him. Charley ran alright, but Sullivan seemed tireless. The outcome of the fight was finally settled by the weather. A heavy rain had soaked the turf on which they were to fight. When it stopped the fighters squared off. Mitchell ran, counter punched when he could, then went down ending the round as John got too close. He landed some good punches, but he took far more. The rain started again. The crowd retreated to the cover of some nearby trees. The rain was cold and needle sharp. The turf soon became a quagmire. The champion later snorted that the ground looked like sheep tracks from Mitchell's evasive tactics. At the thirty ninth round the seconds and the fighters got together. Rather than risk pneumonia, a draw was agreed upon. John's title was safe, but it was a big blow to his pride. If that was not bad enough, prize fighting was also illegal in France. They both went to jail and received medical attention.

Sullivan's old enemy Richard K. Fox, the owner of the famous 'Police Gazette', scoffed at Sullivan's poor showing and declared Jake Kilrain to be the real champion. To prove his point, he had a special championship belt made up and presented it to the new 'title holder'. The good citizens of Boston were furious at this affront. They collected $10,000 dollars and had a gold belt made up, encrusted with 397 diamonds, and presented it to John. Sullivan claimed it made Kilrain's belt look like a dogs collar. Yet John's performance against Mitchell prompted him to risk another title defence. He agreed to meet Kilrain at Richmond, Mississippi on August 8th 1889. It was to be the last heavyweight title fight under the Old London Prize Ring Rules. John almost never made it. His formidable fighting prowess were being corroded by his ever increasing drinking. He was known to have bought a bar and inevitably became his own best customer. Charley Mitchell was aware of this. He had fought a four round draw with Kilrain, and had been impressed enough to become one of his handlers and chief second.

On his first day of training, John sat with his cronies, drinking to the health of his friends and the downfall of his enemies. Training, he informed his handlers, would begin on the morrow. The morrow however, never seemed to arrive. A precious week was lost, while John's toasting seemed to rob him of all sense of reality. Finally someone had enough common sense to fetch the only man who could handle him: William Muldoon, the world's heavyweight wrestling champion. He was the antithesis of Sullivan. He neither smoked, drank or swore. Moreover, he considered the human body to be a temple, never to be desecrated Sullivan was bleary eyed and drunk when Muldoon arrived, and the great wrestler could see he had his work cut out for him. His first act was to lock the liquor cabinet. John attacked him with a baseball bat. Muldoon wrenched it from him and sent the great man off to bed. At first John's training consisted of taking long walks. These walks were extended every day. Soon he was able to run, then took to 'fondling' the dumbbells. Finally Muldoon engaged him in wrestling matches that grew rougher every day. There were times when John's dedication lapsed and Muldoon had to go looking for him in the local bar. But in general he stuck to his guns, as his great strength returned.

On the day of the fight Mitchell looked disconcerted to see the 'Strong Boy' clean shaven, with a flat belly and a malevolent look in his eye. The last battle under the Old London Prize Ring Rules was about to go out in style. Kilrain to his credit, stood up to Sullivan for almost fifteen minutes. He was gradually forced to adopt Mitchell's hit and run tactics, dropping when the champion came too close. John's raw punching power and the benefit of his wrestling matches with Muldoon, were telling on him. As the fight wore on, Mitchell's screaming voice had more power than the brave, badly battered challenger. At the end of the sixty first round his seconds had to carry him back to his corner. By the seventy fifth round the referee marched over, and thrusting his face into Mitchell's bawled, ' You'll kill that man if you send him out again.' With some reluctance,

Mitchell conceded that the fight was over. Before the celebrations could begin, Sullivan was ordered to pay a stiff fine. As for Kilrain, who was literally at death's door, he was held over on a charge of assault and battery. When the celebrations finally started, John went back to toasting his friends and enemies alike, indefinitely. This time there was no Muldoon to check him. He went back to performing on the stage and engaging in undemanding exhibition bouts. His popularity was such that whenever he appeared the theatre tickets were always sold out.

Times however, were changing. A new generation of ambitious young fighters were challenging John's right to call himself the champion. Moreover, this breed was trained under the new Marquis of Queensbury rules. Primarily under the influence of Jem Mace, the game was producing a more scientific kind of fighter. The chief challenger and foremost of this younger generation was the great West Indian, Peter Jackson. Jackson had gone to Australia to join Larry Foley's stable. Foley, a protégé of Mace, had developed some of the greatest talents in the history of the game. This included Jackson himself, the mighty Bob Fitzsimmons and the featherweight legend, Young Griffo. Jackson, as Fitzsimmons was to do a decade later, came to America and began to decimate the heavyweight ranks. He held important wins over Peter Maher and George Godfrey, which certainly entitled him to challenge Sullivan for the crown. When John was told that Jackson was 'really good', it was hardly to his credit that he replied, 'Well, I don't have to fight him. He's black isn't he? 'He then assumed the 'moral high ground' of the day by stating publicly, 'I have never fought a black fighter, and I never will.' Technically speaking, this was true. But in reality, John was not the blatant racist he tried to make himself out to be. In fact in his heyday, John had never shown any objection to meeting black fighters. In September 1881 or 82 Sullivan had trained for a fight with George Godfrey. Both men were stripped and ready for action when the police intervened. On April 20th 1882 John turned up to meet anther black fighter called Johnson. Apparently Johnson thought better of the idea, and never showed up. On May14th 1884 Sullivan was ready to fight Godfrey again. Godfrey claimed he was not ready, but agreed to fight at a later date. This clearly shows that Sullivan had no objection, 'moral' or otherwise, to meeting black fighters. It was more than likely, with his drinking becoming more and more out of control and training a living nightmare, that he did not fancy his chances against Jackson. As a last resort he drew the colour line, knowing full well it was an 'acceptable excuse' for those times.

However, the younger generation would still not leave him alone. Another contender loomed up. A deceptively harmless looking young man named James J. Corbett. Sullivan dismissed him as a 'Dude' and told him gruffly to go out and get himself a reputation. The 'Dude' did just that. He challenged Jackson. Corbett surprised the boxing world by holding this formidable West Indian to a gruelling sixty one round draw. Sullivan now had no choice but to accept the young man's challenge. Then still not taking Corbett as seriously as he should have, he insisted they spar a four round exhibition wearing full evening dress. In New Orleans on September 7th 1892 the reality of the situation was brought home to him. John had forced himself down to a reasonable weight, and even shaved off his moustache to 'show he meant business'. He also assumed it would be business as usual. When all said and done, he still had yet to lose a fight.

In fact Corbett's fight with Jackson had put the finishing touches to a near perfect fighting machine. His combination of speed of hand and foot, ring science, and quick thinking might never have been surpassed in ring history. For the first time in his career John became a victim, unable to cope with the elusive figure before him. All John brought to the ring was the reputation of a once great fighter. Ill trained, ring rusty and past his best, with whatever he might have had left was neutralised by alcohol. Corbett claimed after the fight that he could had ended it any time after the seventeenth round, such was John's strength. He kept him hanging on until the twenty first, when he dropped the old warrior with a powerful right to the jaw. Sullivan crashed to the canvas, face down. A new era was born.

The fight changed John drastically. His hair turned white, and he spoke of himself as an old man. He even went on the wagon, giving lectures on the evil of John Barleycorn. He was revered by those who had the privilege of seeing him fight in his heyday, but it was a very long time before he forgave James J. Corbett, if at all. Yet it was a mark of his greatness and even today , some historians can still be found who consider him to have been unbeatable at his peak.

Gentleman Jim
Posing for his second greatest love: The theatre

Gentleman Jim

Corbett was not one of the more popular champions in fight history, basically because he defeated a living legend. There has also been a tendency among some historians to completely underestimate him. Their findings are in contrast to the historian Nat Fleischer, who saw him in his latter days, and the legendary Jack Johnson, who saw him in his prime.

Corbett was born into an Irish family on September 1st 1866 in San Francisco, far from the Irish poverty belt that existed on the eastern seaboard. He was one of the youngest of twelve children, and he grew into a handsome youth. His mother dearly wished he would become a priest, and most of his opponents dearly wished he had been a more dutiful son and listened to her. Jim, like his elder brothers, chose the prize ring and became a member of the respected Olympic Club. At first he got off to a bad start with an unsympathetic trainer. This instructor took offence at what he considered the young man's arrogance, and then spitefully threw him in with the club's champion. Corbett was unaware of whom he was fighting. He merely thought anyone wearing a beard could not fight. To the trainer's amusement the youngster was knocked out.

Fortunately for Corbett, the instructor was replaced by Professor Watson, who recognised the boy's great potential and helped hone his skills. He took part in countless 'exhibitions' often defeating professional fighters. He also built up many recorded amateur fights. Finally he felt assured enough to quit his job as a bank clerk and join the outlawed ranks of professional fighters.

Corbett's first fights of note were against a neighbourhood rival Joe Choynski, a fast clever boxer with a dangerous right hand. Their first fight took place in a barn, but was interrupted by that occupational hazard, the police. Simultaneously, both fighters and the crowd dispersed in all directions. Corbett had unfortunately broken his thumb, and hoped it would heal before another venue was found. He was out of luck. Five days later the fight was continued on a barge anchored in Benicia bay. At the last moment, someone advised Choynski of Corbett's injury. He consequently dropped his gloves in the water, and suggested they continue the battle with bare fists. Corbett retorted that Choynski could fight bare knuckle if he wished, but he was going to wear gloves. A coachman in the crowd settled the dilemma by throwing his cab gloves at Choynski. They had hard leather strips running down the back. Corbett said he did not care what gloves Choynski wore. He was to regret making that statement. They fought under a blazing sun, with only a spot of shade in the corner of the ring. Both fighters tried to take control of it. Things became worse for Corbett as he wore rubber boxing boots. Blisters came up, popped, then came up again. His feet were soaked in blood. Moreover, it was only time in his career that Corbett was on the wrong end of a sustained beating. He remembered someone at ringside fervently reciting the Lord's Prayer. As Choynski was Jewish, he realised the prayer was for him. Perhaps it worked. In the twenty seventh round he managed to give Choynski an internal nose bleed. As he choked on his own blood, Corbett stepped in with a powerful left hook, a punch some historians claim he invented on the spot, and that decided the matter. They fought a final time in a four round contest with Corbett a clear winner.

Peter Jackson
He could have been the first black heavy weight champion of the world.

A year later, Jim emerged as a top contender when he out pointed Jake Kilrain in New Orleans. He then dared to challenge Sullivan for a shot at the title, and was

gruffly told to get himself a real reputation. A bout with Peter Jackson was consequently arranged. If Sullivan had feigned racialism to avoid fighting Jackson, Corbett's father did not. He threatened to disown his son if the fight went through. It took considerable persuasion on Jim's part to convince his father that the family prestige would be far greater if he became the heavyweight champion of the world. Fighting Jackson, he argued, was the only way to achieve it. With some misgiving, his father relented.

For all his self confidence, Corbett was given little chance against the great West Indian. Jackson was one of the true greats of the game. As stated, his convincing victories over Peter Maher and George Godfrey attested to that. He had the perfect stance, and his mastery of the combination known as the old one two was devastating. He trained down to over two hundred pounds of bone and muscle. Articles were signed and Jackson agreed to meet Corbett at the California Athletic Club in San Francisco on May21st 1891. Jackson certainly realised that he held a psychological advantage. He was heavier and had far greater experience. Corbett tried to neutralise that advantage by trying to psyche him. Before the fight Jackson asked if he could have the blue corner. Corbett said he had no objection. Then Jackson asked if Corbett would mind entering the ring first. It was then he realised Jackson, like most fighters, was a superstitious man. It was the loop hole he had been hoping for. Corbett refused. This apparently minor problem became serious, as neither man would budge. It became a war of nerves. Forty minutes went by. Finally the officials demanded a compromise. Both men would enter the ring at the same time. Reluctantly, they agreed. Eyeing each other, they stood on opposite sides of the ring. Simultaneously, they ducked under the ropes. But as Jackson entered the ring, Corbett swung his body back out. Jackson found himself standing in the ring alone. Corbett was still on the ring apron grinning at him. Jackson was furious. But he possibly may have realised that this young man was not afraid of him. He sent word to his backers that he would knock Corbett out in five rounds. When the bell rang, it was not for want of trying. Corbett remembered in his autobiography, of Jackson trying to one two him to death. As the fifth round loomed up, Jackson sent out word to his backers again. He would knock out Corbett in ten rounds. He was later forced to change that to fifteen. Then he gave up predicting at all. Up to that point it had been a fast and furious contest. Eyewitnesses stated that only after the fifteenth round did the fight begin to slow down. Corbett absorbed more and more of Jackson's considerable repertoire. It certainly honed him into a greater fighter. He claimed he had only to fear Jackson's uppercut, but after six or seven attempts he gave up using it. By the sixty first round the referee stopped the contest, because in his opinion neither man was capable of defending himself. Jackson's seconds were quick to remove his gloves. Corbett admitted he pretended to make a protest. However, his protests became real when Jackson collapsed on his way back to the dressing room. He felt he had been robbed of a sixty second round knockout. Corbett was considered the 'moral winner', and Sullivan had little choice but to put the title on the line. This time however, it was to be under the Marquis of Queensbury rules.

Sullivan, three years ring rusty and a confirmed alcoholic, lost the title in 21 one sided rounds. Corbett as the new champion clearly owed Jackson a rematch. There was even talk about a title defence without the colour bar. Corbett recognised his debt, but it was possible he did not want to go through that hell again. Moreover, there was no boxing association at that time to force the issue. The champion showed more interest in pursuing a career on the stage. It was a profession he was well suited for. He did however, box some benefit exhibitions on behalf of Sullivan, who he privately detested. Apparently, the feeling was mutual. Other than that, he concentrated on acting. The prestige of being the world's champion brought in the crowds, despite his general lack of popularity. After one matinee Corbett came upon a young boy and keenly asked him,' Well, young man, what did you think of my performance?

'Well,' replied the boy, 'it wasn't bad. But then again, it wasn't good.' The champion took this criticism to heart, and worked harder at his stage craft. His challengers would have to wait. It was a mistake many great fighters have made. The lure of the stage and later the cinema often have had a devastating effect on their careers and performances as fighters. From John L. Sullivan to Lennox Lewis, it is a lesson they never seem to learn. However, to keep his hand in, Jim finally chose to defend the title. Peter Jackson was by passed and the ever persistent Charley Mitchell was given a chance. It is often thought that Charlie's talent for verbal abuse earned him a shot at the title. If that was true, it became too much of a good thing.

The fight was held in Jacksonville Florida on January25th 1894. This was six years after Mitchell's controversial bare knuckle draw with Sullivan. Corbett himself was two years ring rusty, yet the fight was brief enough. Charlie's vitriolic tongue knew no bounds. He insulted everything about Corbett he could think of. This included the champion's lovely wife. Corbett, the past master of winding up other fighters, now found himself on the point of blind rage. Charlie easily took the first round and was foolish enough to remind the champion of the fact. Corbett's seconds screamed at him between rounds to control himself, or he would lose the title. Especially, they shrieked, to a man like Mitchell. It worked. Corbett did take control of himself and of Mitchell. He gave the Englishman a fierce shellacking in the second round, and knocked him out cold in the third. Even Charlie's seconds had little sympathy for him. One of them said with a wry smile,' I thought you was gonna get 'im mad, Charlie.' 'I was,' replied Mitchell,' I just didn't think 'e 'ad such an 'orrible temper.'

Jim went back on the stage. About this time the great inventor Thomas Edison, wanted to put a fight on film. First he turned to the old 'Boston Strong Boy', but he wasn't interested. Edison then turned to Corbett. What has come down to us is a magnificent glimpse of the Corbett magic. The fight took place on September 8th 1894 against Peter Courtney. It was held in a specially constructed tin shed called the 'Black Maria'. Each round lasted about a minute and a half before the film ran out and had to be replaced.

Apparently, it was a genuine fight to the finish, or at least until Edison ran out of film. At times Corbett smiled as he slipped Courtney's well aimed punches without moving his feet. Try as he might, Courtney could not land a blow. Corbett finally ended the affair with a blinding right hand to the jaw. It lasted six rounds.

Jim fought an uncomfortable four round draw with the formidable Tom Sharkey, and then decided to call it a day. In a rather high handed manner, he ' gave' the title to Peter Maher. Maher had a good record with knock out wins over Godfrey and Choynski, but in turn he had been knocked out by Peter Jackson and Bob Fitzsimmons. It was decided that Maher should battle Fitzsimmons for the vacant title. Fitzsimmons needed less than a round to settle the dispute. Unpredictably, Corbett became furious and withdrew his retirement pledge. He agreed to defend the title against Fitzsimmons in Carson City Nevada on March 17th 1897.

Those who knew Corbett well said that he made a wonderful friend, but equally, made a deadly enemy. Fitzsimmons was definitely considered an enemy. Fitz admitted that he worried about meeting Corbett because of his rapier like left jab. He was right to have been worried. From the first bell, Fitzsimmons received the thrashing of his life and Corbett did not rely solely on his left jab. Fitz went down in the sixth round, his body covered in red welts. In the seventh round he managed to jolt the champion with a powerful body shot. Jim came back to pile on the pressure. This one sided hammering lessened as the fourteenth round loomed up. Corbett was now beginning to tire, and he was more than aware the fight was to the finish. While he still had the energy, he changed tactics in an attempt to finish off the challenger. It was an understandable but fatal mistake. Fitzsimmons, despite the beating he had absorbed, still possessed his blacksmith's strength. Added to which, his dedicated wife, dressed as a boy, was shouting instructions from his corner. In a most unladylike manner, she bellowed, 'it 'im in the slats Bob.' And like a dutiful husband, he did just that. Corbett was desperate to finish the fight. He went on the offensive and missed with what he hoped to be the finishing blow. For a split second, he was open to a body blow, and Fitz was arguably the most dangerous body puncher in the history of the game. He caught the champion with the Fitzsimmons shift.

Fitz landing the million to one shot that gave him the title

Namely he buried his left fist deep into Corbett's midriff, then caught him on the jaw with the same hand. Corbett dropped, paralysed from the waist down. His legs had temporarily died on him. He frantically crawled towards the ropes, hoping to haul himself back onto his feet. He grabbed at the centre strand, missed, then much like Sullivan had done, fell flat on his face. A new kind of champion had arrived.

Ruby Robert
Showing the raw power that felled more opponents than he could remember

Ruby Robert

If Jim Corbett's dress sense was deceptive as to his formidable fighting skills, then Bob Fitzsimmons appearance was even more deceptive. Standing five foot eleven inches tall, his spindly legs seemed hardly able to bear his powerful torso and iron hard muscular frame. At his fighting peak he weighed 167 lbs and consequently is dismissed by some historians who should know better. Nat Fleischer rated him the 3rd best heavyweight on his all time list. This might seem confusing to some, until one remembers that a heavyweight needs only two basic requisites. 1) That he can hit like a heavyweight and 2) that he can absorb a punch like a heavyweight. Very few fighters under 180 lbs could ever meet both those requirements. Fitzsimmons proved to be one of the few.

Born in Helston Cornwall on June 9th 1862 Fitz's family emigrated to New Zealand when he was nine. His father set up a blacksmith shop, where the child helped out as soon as he was strong enough to hold a hammer. In those days the blacksmiths trade was performed manually, without the aid of electricity. As he grew older, Fitz's natural strength was increased by his daily chores. Among those chores was the task of shoeing half wild horses. He was often thrown on his back or against the wall. He always got up to finish the job. It increased his natural strength and prodigious punching power. This may not seem so obvious in some photographs taken of him, but his opponents testified to it. In keeping with the times, he engaged in many unrecorded fights. Many were bare knuckle affaires under the old London Prize Ring Rules. At the end of his career, Fitz claimed to have engaged in 350 fights all told.

His earliest recorded fight was against another blacksmith known as the 'Timaru Terror'. The 'Terror' lasted less than a round. This victory prompted the good folk of Timaru, to put Fitz's name forward to represent them in a tournament promoted by the great Jem Mace. Fitz flattened four men in a row. Later at the instigation of the crowd, he took on Mace's heavyweight protégé Herbert A. Slade. Mace was grooming him for a shot at John L. Sullivan's world crown. Fitz flattened him too. It has since been claimed that it was not Herbert that Fitz defeated, but his heavyweight look-alike brother. Whichever it was, it was no mean feat as Fitz weighed a mere 140 lbs.

Apparently, when Mace cooled down, he advised the youngster to go Australia and look up Larry Foley. Foley had been another of Mace's protégé's. He was a fighter of little talent, but a trainer of genius. He imbibed Mace's teachings and opened up a fight school that produced some of the greatest names in the history of the sport. Fitz could have done a lot worse. Under Foley, combined with his natural talent and awesome punching power, he developed the skills that carried him to three undisputed world titles.

Fitz started his professional career in Australia by stopping highly rated Dick Ellis in three rounds. However, in order to make some easy money, he later confessed to making a deal with a talented stable mate Jem Hall. Fitz allegedly stopped him in one round, only to be 'knocked out' in turn four months later. He admitted he was paid seventy five dollars for this charade, but it went down in the record books anyway. Fitz then sailed to America with more honest and greater ambitions in view. He stopped the top contender for the middle weight crown Arthur Upham in five rounds. This gave him the right to challenge the original Jack Dempsey for the world's middleweight title. They met in New Orleans on January 14th 1891. The old master put up a stiff fight, but Fitz's overwhelming power was too much for him. He was stopped in thirteen rounds.

Between 1891 and 1894 Fitz held onto the middleweight crown, but he still made his mark among the heavyweights. He stopped the Irish heavyweight champion Peter Maher, in twelve hard fought rounds at catch weight. He next meaningfully stopped his old partner in crime Jem Hall, in four rounds. Then he took on the great Joe Choynski. Choynski was much like Fitz in that he rarely weighed more than 168lbs.yet he established himself as one of the great heavyweights. They met in Boston on June 17th 1894. Fitz had to pick himself up off the deck, but clearly had the best of it when the police stopped the fight. It was recorded as a draw. Fitz then defended his middleweight crown against fellow Australian Dan Creedon, The fight lasted less than two rounds.

Two years later, Jim Corbett decided to give up the heavyweight title and bequeath it to Peter Maher. Fitz felt he had the right to question Corbett's decision, seeing that he had already stopped Maher. The fight crowd agreed with him. A fight was then arranged to contest for the vacant title. Fitz and Maher met for the second time on February 21st 1896 near Langtry Texas. Prize fighting was forbidden in Texas, so the bout was moved across the Rio Grande on the Mexican side of the border. The Texas Rangers sat on the slopes enjoying the fight, waiting to arrest the contestants afterward. This fight was unique in that it was the first championship contest to be put on film. When Fitz heard of this, he approached the promoter with a reasonable request for a percentage of the film rights. The promoter had little time for this. Sitting behind his desk, he barely looked up from his newspaper, and simply told him to close the door behind him, quietly. Fitz did exactly that. The film technicians put up their camera at the ringside. The promoter looked forward to a long drawn out, closely contested battle. It would thrill audiences all over the States, and possibly Europe. Fitz came out and flattened Maher in less than a round.

Despite his victory, no one really considered Fitz the champion. This included Corbett. In a fury he came back to settle the dispute a year later. Fitz was to have one more fight before meeting Corbett. That December he fought Corbett's old adversary, the powerful Tom Sharkey. The referee was the legendary law man and gunslinger Wyatt Earp. This was a good opportunity for Fitz, as getting rid of Sharkey would have consolidated his claim to fight for the real title. He proceeded to do just that. In the eighth round he laid Sharkey low with his much feared solar plexus blow. It was a fair punch, way above the belt. However, this put Wyatt in a difficult position. He and his business associates had bet heavily on Sharkey, and their investment was wreathing in agony on the canvas. Yet Wyatt was the law and the law must be obeyed. To the displeasure of the crowd, he disqualified Fitz. Fitz angrily took a step towards him. Wyatt meaningfully placed his hand on the butt of his Buntline Special. With little choice, Fitz backed off. Decades later, an American T.V.series glorified the exploits of Wyatt with a theme song that ran,

'He cleaned up the country,
The old Wild West country,
He made law and order prevail
For none can deny it, the legend of Wyatt
Forever will live on the trail.'

Whatever trail that was, Fitz certainly got lost wandering down it. For all that, the 'loss' made no difference. Corbett was determined to meet him and consequently lost the title. Jim, as it turned out, was an ungracious loser. Once his legs began to function again, he tried to attack the battered winner. Finally, he cooled down enough to say he merely wanted to congratulate him. Instead he made the threat that unless Fitz fought him again, he would attack him every time he saw him on the street. Fitz replied,' Jim, if you ever hit me again, I will shoot you.' In 1897, that was no idle threat. If nothing else, this should give lie to the 'historians' who claim Corbett could not hit. Fitz fought some of the most powerful punchers in the world, more than once. He would never fight Corbett again. In fact, for the next two years, his whole tenure as champion, he never fought anyone.

Like his great predecessors he engaged in exhibition bouts, then parodied Corbett and went on the stage. He acted in a play that was billed as being, 'In many respects the most unusual play ever written.' Possibly Fitz's lack of acting talent may have contributed to that statement. The efforts from all his challengers failed to get him back in the ring. Corbett especially, must have gone through the same frustration that Peter Jackson must have felt. Fitz finally chose to defend the title against an awkward looking young powerhouse of a man named Jim Jefferies. Jeff, as he was called, was one of the iron men of the ring, perhaps the supreme iron man. He had been one of Corbett's sparring partners for the Fitzsimmons fight. Sitting on a back bench watching the fight, he admitted that he did not think much of either of them.

During the champion's two years of inactivity, Jeff had used the time wisely. He had whipped most of the top contenders including an aging Peter Jackson, to have impressed Fitz enough to give him a chance. Jeff's style resembled that of John L. Sullivan. Then his handlers brought in the legendary world's former welter and current middleweight champion, Tommy Ryan. Apart from being an all time great, Ryan was a brilliant trainer.

He taught Jeff to fight out of a crouch, making him a less vulnerable target for Fitz's iron fists.

Fitz, now going on 37 and carrying two years ring rust, had his work cut out for him. At Coney Island on June 9th 1899, Jeff caused an upset by knocking out the great veteran in eleven rounds. After a stiff fight, a sudden right to the jaw ended the Cornishman's reign. Yet rather than think of retirement, Fitz became revitalised. And like his great predecessor Corbett, he now became obsessed with the idea of regaining the title. The young new champion was happy to oblige them both. Indeed, he offered to take them on both on the same day.

Jim Jefferies
The champions choice

The Boiler Maker

James J. Jefferies came from solid Norman stock. He was born in Ohio, on April 15th 1875, when his family moved out to California, which became his permanent home. Jeff was a natural athlete and a great sprinter. He was able to run a hundred yards in ten seconds flat, which may have been something of a world record at the time. His greatest asset as a fighter was an almost inhuman ability to absorb a punch, equalled only by his ability to hit like a mule. He was known, with his hands properly protected, to have buried a six inch nail into a plank of wood with one blow. In his youth he worked as a boilermaker. And like Fitz at the anvil, all manual labour at that time, was done by hand without the aid of electricity. Jeff's break came when he was noticed by Harry Corbett, a Californian sportsman. Corbett felt he would be a great help to Jim Corbett (no relation) in his forthcoming defence against Fitzsimmons. His bear like strength would be more than useful to the dashing champion. At times he became the butt of the camp wits, due to his awkward movements. However, the champion, albeit in his own interest, gave the youngster something of a fistic education. In part, it helped mould him into the great fighter he was to become.

Jeff now started his own climb towards the championship. The fight game took notice with Jeff's controversial 20 round draw against top liner Gus Ruhlin. Ruhlin took a bad beating, culminating with his being knocked down as the fight drew to a close. The bell saved him. The referee drew the displeasure of the crowd by declaring the fight a draw. Then Jeff battled Joe Choynski. Despite holding a forty pound advantage, Jeff was lucky to hold on to a draw. In those days gum shields had yet to be invented. Choynski caught Jeff in the mouth, burying his upper lip between his front teeth. It was painfully extracted. This said something of Jefferies outstanding ability to take a punch, because Choynski could really hit.

The next big name was the aging master Peter Jackson. He lasted three rounds, going down twice in the second. This was really a prestige fight for Jeff, as Jackson was by this time merely a shell of his former self. Then came Tom Sharkey. He stood up to Jeff for round after round, going down in the eleventh. He came back strongly to lose a close twenty round decision. His final battle before his title fight with Fitz was against a tough but outclassed Bob Armstrong.

Under the guidance of Tommy Ryan, Jeff became champion with a stunning 11th round knockout over Fitzsimmons. And unlike his great predecessors, he was neither shy nor slow in defending the title. With some respect, he gave his old adversary Tom Sharkey another chance. The respect was justified. They met at Coney Island on November 3rd 1899 in one of the most brutal battles ever contested for the crown. In fact, both were much improved fighters, which added to the drama. It was also filmed, although some of it is barely discernable. Powerful arc lights were placed just above their heads to add to their considerable discomfort. Jeff had Sharkey down in the second round for a short count. He seemed in control, when in the seventeenth round the challenger almost turned the fight around. Jeff retaliated by breaking three of Sharkey's ribs with a tremendous body blow. One rib pierced the skin and Sharkey was forced to hold his glove over it for protection. Jeff, determined to keep his title, shifted his attack to the head and gave Sharkey a cauliflower ear. The challenger responded with a head butt to split Jeff's forehead open. In the final round, Jeff's left glove came off in breaking out of a clinch. As the referee replaced it, Sharkey charged forward to be caught by Jeff's taped fist. As the glove was replaced, the final bell rang. Some of the crowd stubbornly thought Sharkey had won, but most had no qualms when the referee George Siler raised Jeff's hand as the winner and still champion. The brave challenger was taken to hospital.

On April 6th 1900 Jefferies despatched Jack Finnegan in 55seconds, to hold the fastest knockout in heavyweight championship history. One month later he caught a tarter in defending the title against his old boss James J. Corbett. Jim's fortunes had not been progressing well. Fitzsimmons had steadfastly kept his promise in refusing to meet him again. Then on November 22nd 1898, he had engaged in a controversial bout with the rugged Tom Sharkey. It was not a good fight for Corbett. He showed only flashes of his former self, while Sharkey caught him with blows no one had ever come close to landing before. As Jim started to get back into the fight, one of his second's Connie Mcvey, climbed into the ring as the fight was in progress. The referee 'Honest' John Kelly promptly stopped the proceedings. He called off all bets and awarded the fight to Sharkey on a foul. The true story behind all this has never been unearthed. Historians have only come to their own conclusions. It is possible that Corbett's poor performance may have prompted Jeff to have accepted him as a challenger. Although in truth, he never looked for an easy option when it came to defending the title.

On May 11, 1900 at Coney Island, Corbett finally got his second chance, and he certainly made the best of it. What ensued was one of the greatest battles for the heavyweight crown. Scheduled for 25 rounds, Corbett gave the performance of his life. As the betting underdog, it was something no one could have predicted. He treated the champion as though he was a bumbling novice. Jefferies, who in reality was much faster than many historians are willing to give him credit for, could barely cope with Corbett's ring craft. The champion, a fighter of titanic strength, who could conceivably have taken the challenger out with one punch from either hand, could do nothing. Corbett's dazzling footwork, counter punching and ring science was master class. Corbett's youth seemed to have returned. He was by no means the same fighter who had struggled with Sharkey. Had the fight been fought under a modern time limit, Corbett would have been the first man to have regained the heavyweight title. As the rounds slipped away, Jeff became more and more convinced that the title was lost. Unfortunately for Corbett, he became convinced of the same thing. So much so that he broke his own concentration. At the end of the 22nd round, he sat on his stool and let his mind wander. In his autobiography, he stated how he could hear the newsboys on the street greet him with the words,' Hi ya champ.' This reverie was interrupted by the sound of the bell for the 23rd round. The fight was not over yet. Outclassing Jefferies was not easy. Corbett had made it look easy. Suddenly the champion trapped him on the ropes. The knockout blow was so clean that Corbett found himself sitting on his stool with no memory of what had happened. He was actually waiting for the next round to begin. His chief second, realising this, said he was heartbroken to have to tell him that he had been knocked out. Corbett certainly deserved a rematch, and he got one. But the beating Jefferies sustained was so severe that he kept Corbett waiting for another three years. Yet Jeff continued to be a fighting champion. Six months later he cleared his slate with Gus Ruhlin, flattening him in just five rounds.

Then on July 25th 1902 the mighty Fitzsimmons was given his chance. In a blood soaked battle, Jeff came closer to losing the title than he did against Corbett. Fitz, despite his age was still a great fighter. After he lost the title, he seemed to go out of his way to prove it. Indeed he went on a knock out rampage among the top contenders. Jim Daley, Ed Dunkhorst, Gus Ruhlin all suffered knock outs at Fitz's hands. Then, embarrassing to Jefferies, Fitz went on to flatten his old adversary, Tom Sharkey, and he needed less than two rounds to do it.

Jeff signed to meet the old master in San Francisco on July 25 th 1902. In a real sense, an incident happened at the weigh in that may have been the deciding factor of the fight. Fitz, seemingly in a jovial mood, acknowledged Jeff's near inhuman ability to absorb a blow. He half jokingly said that this time he would soak his hand tapes in plaster of Paris. Jeff, apparently a man of little humour, defiantly told him to go ahead. There is strong evidence that is exactly what he did. If so, he added to his own destruction. At the age of thirty eight, Fitz proved to be as sharp as ever. This time Jeff's crouching style was not an obstacle to his murderous punching power. He dominated the fight, cutting the champion's face to the bone, braking his nose and gashing him badly above the eyes. Yet Fitz, who never had trouble with his hands, indeed he affectionately referred to them as his bony sledgehammers, now found they were broken. Jeff, in agony, threw himself at his tormentor. He drove a terrific left hand to the stomach, followed by a crunching left hook to the jaw. He was still the champion. For all that, many observers still felt Fitz to be the best heavyweight in the world.

Yet his great days were not quite over, for at the age of 41 he went on to win the newly created light heavyweight championship of the world. The fight was unique in that it was a points decision. The old master had finally lost his punch, but had enough ring craft to take the new title. On retirement, like many other great fighters, he became a man of the cloth, preaching good will to all men. He is still revered as one of the legends of the ring.

Jeff defended the title on two further occasions. He finally gave his old mentor James J. Corbett another chance, but Jim had nothing left but his courage. He was stopped inside ten rounds. Then during an exhibition match, Jeff was allegedly knocked down for the first time in his career by a tough miner called Jack Munro. Some observers said it was merely a slip. Whatever it was, the promoter Jack Curly was not one to let an opportunity go by. He stopped the show, and trumped up enough interest to warrant a title fight. On August 26th 1904 Jeff flattened Munro inside two rounds then decided to call it a day. He selected Marvin Hart and former world light heavyweight champion Jack Root to contest for the vacant title. As far as he was concerned, he was finished with the fight game. Unfortunately for him fate had other ideas.

Tommy Burns
A brave but outclassed champion

Marvin Hart, Tommy Burns and Their Times.

The official ownership of the title was settled on July3rd 1905 in Reno. Marvin Hart came from behind on points to overpower Jack Root in twelve rounds. Jefferies, acting as referee, stepped in to save Root from further punishment. Hart may have been the official titleholder, but he was hardly the best heavyweight in the world. For all that, he does deserve some genuine credit. With Jefferies gone, the most gifted heavyweight in the world was undoubtedly Jack Johnson, a Texas Afro American. Paradoxically, Hart won a controversial points win over him four months before he won the title. It was this victory that encouraged Jefferies to consider Hart as one of the contenders.

The truth of the Hart Johnson fight might never be known. On July 28th 1905 in San Francisco they battled to a 20 round points decision. Johnson seemed lethargic, content to outbox his man for11 or 15 rounds. Eyewitnesses vary. The seconds of both men exhorted their fighters to put more into it. Apparently Hart did just that. He attacked vigorously for the rest of the fight. Some accounts say he not only gave Johnson a pounding, but actually staggered him before the final bell. This was enough for the referee to ignore the fact that Johnson had won most of the early rounds, and gave the verdict to Hart. Paradoxically, Johnson not only admitted he was beaten fairly but that Hart was the best men he ever met. Historians have much to ponder on.

It was known that while Jefferies was still champion, Johnson personally went to the bar Jeff owned, and challenged him to a title fight. Standing behind the counter before his cronies, Jeff mocked him. He told him there was a cellar down below, and invited Johnson to go down there with him. They would lock the door and fight. Whoever unlocked the door would be the champion. Johnson declined the offer and walked out. He was also said to have badgered Hart for a fight, calling him a coward if he refused to meet him. Hart did agree to fight him and his victory in San Francisco at least gave him some credibility for his bout with Root.

Marvin did not retain the title for long. A mere seven months in fact. Yet in a sense, he was one of the more fortunate men to have held the crown. Primarily because he never took the whole thing too seriously. He never worried about being the greatest, or who was coming up to challenge his reputation. His only grievance was against the man he lost the title to: Tommy Burns. He felt Burns had not made a real fight of it, but stole the fight from under him. Their 20 round bout took place in Los Angeles on February 23rc 1906. Hart may have been a more powerful fighter than some critics give him credit for, because Burns treated him warily, careful not to mix it with him. He edged out a points decision to become the new titleholder. Hart boxed on for another four years before going into business and living out a happily married life.

Hart's successor gained far more notoriety. Tommy Burns was really a French Canadian named Noah Brusso. And to this day, at 5ft 7ins.he remains the shortest man ever to hold the title. He was really a magnificent light heavyweight, who packed a stiff enough punch strong enough to take out some world class heavyweights. To prove it he knocked out the more than useful Fireman Jim Flynn in 15 rounds. Next came two controversial bouts with the all time great Philadelphia Jack O'Brien. Their first bout ended in a twenty round draw. Some historians feel this was an arranged decision. In the rematch O'Brien, who seemed very free with his 'confessions', claimed he paid Burns to lose the title to him. Apparently, Burns double crossed him. He took the bribe, won the decision, and then had the cheek to claim O'Brien's world light heavyweight title. After Burns lost the title O'Brian out pointed him in a genuine contest.

It may be worthwhile to say something of O'Brien here. He seems to be judged harshly over his signed confession that most of his fights were faked. His confession notwithstanding, Nat Fleischer, who saw him fight often, rated him the second best light heavyweight of all time. Charley Rose rated him the third. Yet O'Brien's confession was well known to them. It appears he was a controversial, if not testy individual, with little liking for press and sports writers. He often sarcastically said things they wanted to hear. For example he said he would never fight a black fighter, yet his record is crammed with black fighters, often great fighters no one else wanted to fight. At the hint that a fight he had engaged in was fixed, he went to the other extreme and claimed that all his fights had been fixed. For all that, O'Brian was greatly respected in the fight world by his fellow boxers. This controversial character was also known to play the violin very well.

In all Tommy Burns defended the title 11times, which was a record up to that time. At first he avoided his real and most dangerous chief challenger, Jack Johnson. And unlike his great predecessor Peter Jackson, Johnson was determined not to let the infamous colour bar prevent him from claiming what he felt was rightfully his. Burns went on a world tour, and eventually put the title on the line against Johnson at Rushcutters Bay in Sydney Australia on December the 26th 1908. The racial slurs and colour bar which had tormented Johnson for so long, now found a release. Johnson wanted more than the title, he wanted revenge. Burns, a great light heavyweight no doubt, was outclassed. Johnson dragged the fight out, punishing the smaller man, until the police blocked out the cameras and stopped the fight. Despite the moral indignation of the authorities, no fouls had been committed. Jack Johnson duly became the first black fighter to be crowned the undisputed heavyweight champion of the world.

Burn v Johnson fight

Jack Johnson. Defensive genius.

'Lil Artha'

Johnson's climb to the top was particularly tortuous. As a youngster he was known to have participated in 'Battle Royals' whereby six fighters would enter the ring blindfolded, for the amusement of the crowd. The slightest touch would trigger off a quick fire response. When the last two men were left, the blindfolds were removed, and they would contest for the prize money. This often consisted of loose change being thrown into the ring. Mixed fights in the Southern states were illegal, just as boxing itself. A man would have to be very dedicated or very desperate to follow such a profession.

Like all youngsters Jack had his idol. In his case it was Corbett. As a fourteen year old, he took a beating from some yobbish youths for predicting Gentleman Jim would take the title from Sullivan. Later, when he turned professional, his gifts were appreciated by the original Joe Walcott, and the great master took him under his wing for a while. Jack had built up a good record with over thirty fights under his belt. After two years, he was finally able to obtain a fight with a big name fighter, Joe Choynski. Choynski was really getting fights on his reputation by that time. He was certainly ready to be taken by an ambitious youngster. Following a losing streak and desperate for money, Choynski travelled to Johnson's home in Galveston, Texas. Prize fighting, and especially mixed matches were illegal, but both men were willing to take the risk. Unfortunately for Jack's ambitions, it sometimes happens that an old timer will get some of his old spark back. In the second round, Choynski flattened the youngster with a devastating right hand to the temple. The police, watching the battle, and seeing Johnson was hardly going to get up, stopped the proceedings. The presiding judge, with a wonderful show of equality threw both men in the same cell, occupied with several other felons.. They were given a month's detention, but permitted to go home in the evening. In the daytime they entertained the other inmates with friendly sparring matches. Choynski predicted a great future for the promising youngster.

With the retirement of Jim Jefferies, the black domination of the sport began, even though they were barred from contesting for its richest prize. A fighter hones his skills on basically who he has been in there with. And Johnson cut his teeth on some of the finest talent in the history of the game. Namely Joe Jeanette, Sam Mcvey and Sam Langford. Johnson overcame them all. His battle with Langford in 1906 was almost as controversial as the second Dempsey Tunney fight. Some reports say the fight was so gruelling that

Johnson would never fight him again. Yet Nat Fleischer's father in law, who saw the fight, claimed it was an easy win for Johnson. Press reports of the time seem to agree with that. Whatever the facts, these two men developed an implacable hatred for one another. It became entwined in the history of the sport.

Sam Langford, another great tragic master who was denied his chance.

Standing only 5ft 7 inches and a half, with a barrel chest, long arms and a killer punch, Langford's record reads like a who's who of boxing. He fought many world champions at different weights, but none, black or white, were foolish to put their titles on the line against him. Since his loss to Johnson, Sam put on weight, increased his already formidable punching power, and battled any heavyweight who would dare enter the ring against him.

When Tommy Burns started on his world tour, Johnson and Langford were close behind. If Tommy had a choice against which of them he would defend the title, it was tantamount to asking if he wished to be shot or hung. Burns incidentally, was no coward. When he did fight Johnson he went out with a champion's courage. Burns set sail for Australia. Johnson was keen to follow him, but was short of funds. The British National Sporting Club stepped in and offered to pay Johnson's fare. But only on condition that should he win the title, he would return to England and defend it against Langford. Johnson gave his hand and his solemn word. And that was the closest Sam ever got to a chance at the world title.

As stated, Johnson took the title from Burns in Australia. Langford and the British National Sporting Club waited for Johnson to take the next boat back to England. Instead he took the first available boat to San Francisco. At first Johnson considered breaking the colour bar by defending against an undemanding black fighter, but he changed his mind. He fought a non title fight against the future movie star Victor Mclaglen, whom he permitted to last the route. He also fought a six round draw with Philadelphia Jack O' Brien. The short duration of the fight suited O'Brien, who fought brilliantly. Johnson then made a title defence against the world's middleweight champion, the great Stanley Ketchel. Like most of Johnson's title defences, this was something of a farce. Before the fight, pictures of Ketchel were taken where he wore two sets of clothing, to make him appear bigger. Ketchel always fought a few pounds under the middleweight limit. In fact a deal was made, in which both parties agreed to a 20 round no decision fight that would last the distance. It would be filmed, a lot of money would change hands, and no one would get hurt. Johnson felt he had kept his part of the bargain by not hurting Ketchel, too much.

This was not exactly true. Johnson carried a tremendous weight advantage. He constantly cut Ketchel's face open. Ketchel's corner men would mop up the blood, then send him out for another round. Johnson's great defensive skills held him in good stead. He often tried to humiliate the challenger by exchanging a few witticisms with those sitting at ringside. Ketchel however, had two great assets. He had unlimited courage, and a right hand worthy of a heavyweight. We know this because he caught Johnson with it in the twelfth round. Now it was the champion's turn to feel humiliated. He had been knocked down by middleweight, and he was hurt. He was also very angry. Ketchel backed off to get a good run to finish him off. Johnson rose in a cold fury and met him half way. With the collision of their respective weights Ketchel was knocked cold. Although he looked dead to the world, he raised himself close to the end of the referee's count, and started to get up under his own steam. It was said that later in Johnson's dressing room, the champion pulled Ketchel's front teeth out of his glove, where they were embedded. Apparently, they became good friends, and Ketchel was said to have been the only white man Johnson ever liked. Yet their friendship notwithstanding, when films of the fight were shown across America, race riots broke out. As many as eight people were killed.

It was a high price to pay for a prize fight, and an intended fake one at that. It was then that the writer Jack London started the drums rolling for a 'Great White Hope'. It was a vain quest. It would be another eight years before America would produce a white fighter of Johnson's stature. And if White America could not look forward, even more idiotically, it felt no choice but to look back. Jack London, who had been something of a boxer himself, should have known better. But he demanded nothing less than the great Jim Jefferies himself come back and restore the pride and the title to the white race. Had anyone bothered to ask Jefferies about this, they would have found that he was not interested. He was enjoying the prestige of an undefeated former champion, and doing very nicely on his alfalfa farm. He certainly did not need Jack Johnson. Unfortunately, White America felt it needed him. He was hounded by the press, religious groups, and women who pleaded the cause for his return. The latter were even prepared to offer him a white feather, the symbol of cowardice, should he refuse. Between the endless harassment and the large amount of money that promoter Tex Rickard offered him, Jeff finally gave in. Much against his better judgement, he gave way. He even gave the 'right kind' of statements to the press, although it was not known how much of this they put into his mouth. When all said and done, he had never been beaten. Possibly, that feeling may have stayed with him. However, there were to be no warm up fights to shake off six years of ring rust. This was to be a one off.

Once in training, Jeff expended whatever was left of his once great strength in getting down to a reasonable fighting weight. Corbett turned up to partly supervise his training. Choynski, who had once held Jeff to a gruelling twenty round draw, and knocked Johnson out nine years before, also turned up to relive the past. He sparred a filmed session with the ex champion. Even old John L. Sullivan paid them a visit. With an experience eye, he took one look at Jefferies and declared the fight must be a fake. Corbett took extreme offence to this and a second Sullivan Corbett fight seemed imminent. The fight of course was not a fake. It was just supreme foolishness. For Johnson it became business as usual. Even more than the Burns Ketchel fights, it was a case of one man beating another who had no chance at all.

Johnson, who had seen Jefferies in his prime, fought a very cautious first round. He had to see just how much Jefferies had left. In the second round he surprised Jefferies by engaging in a pushing contest. Jefferies gave ground. He had nothing left. Johnson flashed a big grin and went to work. It was payback time. As with the Burns fight, Johnson could have finished it any time he chose. Instead he dragged it out, taunting Jefferies, talking to ringsiders, and even exchanging some words with Corbett, who tried to distract him. Only once did Jefferies get something of his old spark back. He caught the champion off balance, and pulled him onto a vicious left hook to the ribs. Johnson gasped, but his ribs were not broken. The beating continued. One of Jefferies seconds tried to enter the ring in the hope of a face saving disqualification. Johnson turned and angrily chased him out. Then the second threw in the sponge and Rickard, also acting as referee, stopped the slaughter. The fight had gone on for fifteen rounds. Predictably, when films of the fight were shown nationwide, race riots broke out all over the country. They were far more severe than after the Ketchel fight. The death toll was also far greater. Mostly Afro Americans died, but there were white fatalities too. Louis Armstrong remembered as a ten year old, being chased down the street by a mob of furious white youths. Some whites were beaten up by a white racist mob for coming to the aid of a black man. Millions of dollars worth of property went up in smoke and looting was rampant by both races.

After the fight, Johnson and his entourage, which included Nat Fleischer, travelled to New York to celebrate in the Harlem night spots. Al Jolson covered the fight as a reporter for the July issue of Variety. He wrote so positively of Johnson's performance, stating that he could have beaten Jefferies even in his prime. In response, the owner of Leroy's Black Cabaret in Harlem permitted Jolie to be the only white man to enter the place. The race riots seemed to have had little effect on Johnson or the white promoters who distributed the fight films. Johnson, if anything, went further by flaunting his relationships with white women. The great bantam weight boxer George Dixon had also taken a white wife, but he had none of the trouble Johnson had. Johnson's wife was a beautiful, vulnerable woman called Etta. Gunboat Smith knew the Johnson's well. He earned Jack's respect as a sparring partner by knocking his boss out of the ring on his first day at work. According to Smith's eyewitness account, Johnson enjoyed berating his wife in public. He admitted he was tempted to throw a punch at Johnson himself. Etta also received hate mail from the white racist brigade. Finally, isolated with little or no support from her husband, Etta took her life. Jack took another white wife twelve weeks later. It is debatable how much of an effect Etta's suicide and the combined death toll from the race riots had on him. He could claim to have done nothing wrong. He had proved his right to the heavyweight crown, and he had merely married the woman he loved. Yet he had humiliated and tormented white opponents in fights he could not lose, and part of that torment and humiliation was metered out to Etta. On the one hand, Johnson's rebellion was understandable, but it is not unreasonable to assume that he was working out some deep seated personal revenge. In reaction to Johnson, the cry for a great white hope became more intense, so did the colour bar. Ironically Johnson himself refused to defend the title against black fighters. Had he done so it might have made a dent in the colour bar. His most deserving challenger Sam Langford, detested Johnson much for the same reason Peter Jackson had detested Sullivan.

Jack managed one more title defence in the states. He stopped, or more to the point, the police stopped his fight with Fireman Jim Flynn in the 9th round. The authorities then charged him with the Mann act I.E. 'Taking an under aged female over the state line for immoral purposes'. He fled the country eventually turning up in Paris. This city was a virtual haven for black fighters. Sam Langford often fought there and became Picasso's favourite fighter. Unfortunately, no enterprising promoter could get Johnson to fight him. Eventually Jack did defend against a black fighter. Low on money, he took on Jim Johnson in Paris on December19th 1913.Jack broke his arm in the tenth round and could not continue. The French let him keep his title and called the fight a draw. His final successful defence was against a fellow American Frank Moran. The fight went twenty rounds, with Jack taking the decision.

It is claimed that the American authorities secretly offered Johnson a deal. Namely, he would get a reprieve from a pending jail sentence if he would lose the title. He would be allowed to return home and all would be forgiven. This has never actually been proven. Johnson was still very wary of returning to the states. However, a championship fight was arranged in nearby Cuba. Jack apparently chose the challenger himself. He was not a particularly gifted fighter; In fact he had lost a decision to Johnson's old sparring partner, Gunboat Smith. This was a giant cowboy from Pottawatomie Kansas called Jess Willard. Willard had very little championship qualities. He stood just over six and a half feet, possessed a powerful punch, which he rarely used, took a punch well, and had endless courage. And that was it. He loathed training almost as much as he loathed the fight game. He was in it solely for the money. The idea of a fix is to be further doubted because Jack personally chose Willard, aware of his lack of talent. Moreover, if Johnson had agreed to take a dive, the authorities must have had little faith in his promise. Willard was given the benefit of expert trainers. They worked on Jess's main weakness, his legs. The fight was scheduled for a long drawn out 45 rounds. The idea behind this is that a younger stronger man would outlast the aging champion.

Yet talk on the fix persisted. The great Ted 'Kid' Lewis, who helped Johnson prepare for the fight, claimed the fix was an open secret. He also admired Johnson's supreme defensive skills. He claimed Johnson was so good he was unable to get past his guard. Yet the rumours notwithstanding, Willard was still a very worried man. He certainly believed the fight to be on the level. He was also aware that he was not in Johnson's class. April 5th 1915 was a blazing hot day in Havana Cuba. As the fight started it seemed that Willard was about to join Burns and Jefferies, but that was not Johnson's intention. He did not set out to taunt and humiliate Willard. He simply tried to knock him out. Jess had been told to stay away and let the champion come to him. It was sound advice, although the challenger still took a real beating. Johnson willingly went on the offensive, and it was all Willard could do to stay on his feet. His ability to absorb a punch was the only thing that kept him in the fight. By the tenth round Willard was bleeding with his ribs badly battered. Talk of a fix was nonsense. Johnson was clearly trying for a knockout. By the twentieth round the champion had finally tired himself out, and the tide of the battle changed. Willard was then instructed to move forward. It was only Johnson's supreme defensive skills that stopped him from going under. As the rounds passed and the terrific heat sapped Johnson's energy, Willard's prospects of victory grew stronger. At the start of the 26th round Jack motioned for his wife to leave the arena. Then a vicious combination to the body then a powerful right to the jaw ended Johnson's reign as champion. He lay flat on his back allegedly shielding his eyes from the sun. This became one of the most famous pictures in the history of the sport. Jack later claimed this photograph proved the fight had been fixed. However, if one looks carefully at the picture, one sees that he is not shielding his eyes. The sun is shining straight in his face. The shadow is resting on the top of his head. Moreover,if there had been a deal, the authorities went back on their word. When Jack returned to the states he was sent to jail to serve out his sentence.

Nat Fleischer was not alone in considering Johnson to be the greatest heavyweight he ever saw. And despite the advent of Dempsey, Louis, Marciano and Ali, he never changed that opinion. Like Peter Jackson, he possessed the perfect stance, and vied with Corbett as a defensive genius. He had a punishing left jab and a devastating uppercut. He claimed his opponents really knocked themselves out as he hit them with their own weight.

In this day of political correctness he is hailed as a hero, and in many ways he was. Yet in his wake, he made it difficult, if not impossible for a black fighter to get a chance to challenge for the heavyweight crown. He even drew the colour line himself, ignoring his most deserving challengers: especially Sam Langford. In a perverse way he accepted the white man's authority by stating he wanted to be the only black man to hold the heavyweight crown. Langford went to his grave hating Johnson for denying him his rightful chance. The next generation of fighters, white as well as black, suffered from his influence in different ways. White champions who were willing to fight anyone, had their reputations tarnished, while black fighters stood no chance at all.

Yet there is a story for which he should be remembered. While still champion, Jack was speeding through one of the southern states in a fast car. A racist cop tore after him, and made him pull over. 'You broke the speed limit,' he cried lividly.' 'I'm fining you fifty dollars on the spot.' Jack silently handed him a hundred dollar bill. A bit lamely, the cop said,' I haven't got any change.' 'Never mind,' replied Lil Artha. 'Keep it, 'cos I'm comin' back the same way.'

Jess Willard
He hated training and the fight game, yet became a champion

Big Jess

Most, if not all historians would agree that Jess Willard as a fighter, could not have carried Jack Johnson's bucket. Yet in 1915 white America hailed him as a national hero. The legendary Indian fighter, buffalo hunter and gunslinger, who fought alongside Wyatt Earp at the OK corral, now turned sportswriter, Bat Masterson, thought Jess to be the greatest fighter who ever lived. After a time, the slightly bewildered champion began to believe it himself. It almost certainly had a hand in his undoing.

Despite Jess holding the official title, everyone knew the real champion was Sam Langford. That however, was no concern of Willard's. He defended the title the following year against the dependable Frank Moran in Madison Square Garden. The fight left such a bad taste that the authorities threatened to ban boxing in New York. The champion went back to resting on his laurels. The next year the black domination of the sport was broken. Fred Fulton, a fighter as tall as Willard with an immaculate left jab and a devastating right hand, defeated the mighty Langford, stopping him in seven rounds. Even the great Harry Greb, who successfully entered the light heavyweight and heavyweight ranks, was said to have steered clear of him. Langford sportingly admitted he thought Fulton would beat Willard. The champion, sensing a big money fight, started to think it over. A year crawled by, and then disaster. Fulton was destroyed in eight seconds by a tough as nails ex hobo, a product of the hobo jungles that were spreading across America. Some called this newcomer 'The Manassa Mauler', others 'The 'Tiger Man'. But no matter what they called him, he revitalised the game and carved his name in the history books. Yet Jess, convinced in his own omniscience, was unable to take him seriously. At a mere 6ft 1ins. and weighing between 180-186lbs. Jess thought him too small. When they finally met, their battle, while it lasted, was always remembered as 'The Massacre of Toledo.'

The Massacre of Toledo

Jack Dempsey
Every fighters nightmare

The Manassa Mauler

To this day, years after his death, Dempsey's name inspires love, adulation, hatred and envy. Many fight writers will sit for hours poring over his fight movies, exalting his powers, or insisting he was not all he was cracked up to be. More often than not, the reminisces of those who actually saw him, or fought against him, are very different from the verdict of many of these lap top critics. For all that, he remains one of the true immortals of the game. Gerry Cooney said after his death in 1983, 'To have faced him in his prime must have been a living nightmare'. Indeed, one of Jack's last words to his wife before he died were,' Honey, 'I'm too mean to die.' Many of his opponents would have agreed with that.

Despite the warmth of a loving family, a restless ambition pushed him into the savage hobo jungles from the tender age of sixteen. With little education, he soon realised that the best, if not the only way to survive, was with his fists. He learned his craft the hard way. The hungry youngster would enter a bar and state confidently, 'I can't sing, an' I can't dance, but I can lick any son of a bitch in the house,' then add lamely,' For a buck.' Often the challenge would be taken up, and a hat would be passed around. Other times bare knuckle fights would be more organised, and unlike many other great fighters, Dempsey never had trouble with his hands. Most of the time he won. But there were times when he didn't. On one such occasion he was knocked out, shoved in a wheel barrow then dumped on the garbage site on the outskirts of town. His basic problem was usually where his next meal was coming from. When the famous lecturer Dale Carnegie gathered material for a book, he asked the aging Dempsey how he coped when things got tough. Dempsey replied that from his hobo days he always had faith. Although he was not a practicing Mormon, he did believe in it. When he raided a garbage can and found something to eat, he always gave thanks to God. He always had that element of gratitude. This was probably why in later years, his erratic manager Jack 'Doc' Kearns, thought he was stupid. Gratitude in Kearns was something that was totally lacking. Dempsey's hobo days moulded him both physically and mentally into the fighter he was to become. And like his great predecessor Bob Fitzsimmons, he did not know exactly how many fights he had had. When he turned professional at nineteen, if he lost or drew with a fighter, he was always eager to fight them again until he mastered them. He was a most enterprising youth, who while active himself, also managed other fighters. For most part he was a consistent winner with a rare loss or draw. He built up a reputation as a tenacious knock out artist, who carried dynamite in both fists with a chin like granite. When he stopped a huge black fighter called 'The Boston Bearcat' inside one round, he decided after a few more fights to try the big time in New York. Part of his decision was based on the assumption that the Bearcat had once lasted twenty rounds with Dempsey's idol, Sam Langford. When he got there all he found was trouble. He fell into the clutches of a mercenary manager called John the Barber. John was well connected in the fight scene, but he was no talent scout. He also had a heart like an ice cream cone. He offered the young hopeful a fight with Langford himself. Or if he preferred Joe Jeanette, or the fighter who had fought both Jack Johnson and Jess Willard for the title and neither had been able to knock him out, Frank Moran. Guided more by common sense than fear, Dempsey turned them all down. This refusal tried what little patience John had. He threatened the youth, that if he refused his final opponent, John Lester Johnson, he would make sure he would never fight in New York again.

With some misgiving, Dempsey took the fight. There a conflicting stories about what actually happened. Dempsey remembered Johnson busting three of his ribs in the third round. Despite fearing the splinters would go into his heart and kill him, the youngster refused to quit. On the contrary, he took the fight to Johnson. One newspaper reported, 'Johnson looked tired at the end of the fight from punches he had received around the head and body.' Dempsey himself, feeling the pain in his ribs, thought Johnson had the better of it. It was a 'no decision' fight, relying on newspaper verdicts. It went down as a draw. It is hard to gage how badly Dempsey's ribs were broken. The fight took place at the Harlem Sporting Club on 14th July 1916. His next recorded fight was on the 28th September of the same year when he flattened Young Hector in three rounds.

As there was nothing in writing between John the Barber and Dempsey, their 'relationship' seems to have dissolved. Most of Dempsey's purse went on hospital bills, and no doubt the Barber took the rest. It a time of discouragement, and things got even worse. Dempsey came up with an even bigger name fighter than Johnson. This was Fireman Jim Flynn, who had battled both Burns and Johnson for the heavyweight crown, not to mention Langford. It resulted in the only official knockout loss on Dempsey's record. He went out in one round. Some historians suspected the fight was a fake. Dempsey denied it, but the suspicion still remains. Sometime later he turned up as a sparring partner for another world contender, Carl Morris. Yet the youth seemed to have lost his direction. One day while eating in a bar, he broke up a fight between some men over a game of cards. The man he rescued asked for his address, which Dempsey gave him. In fact he knew the man vaguely, as the fight manager Jack Kearns. He remembered him because he had once knocked out one of his boy's. For all that he dismissed the incident. He considered himself finished with the fight game.

A short time later he received a letter from San Francisco. Kearns offered to be his manager. Dempsey replied that if he sent him a ticket he would come, but he still never took the offer seriously A week later he received a ticket in the post. Despite the fact that these two men came to loathe each other, the greatest fighter manager team was born. Dempsey even nick named Kearns the 'Doc' meaning he would always obey the' doctors orders'. Kearns would not have it any other way. Yet he knew his stuff, and first he had to be sure about his new fighter. He threw him in with another world class fighter, Fat Willie Meehan. They fought a fast four rounder. Dempsey lost a close decision. Next Kearns put him in with another top liner, Al Norton. It was a slight improvement. The bout ended in a four round draw. Kearns threw him back in with Fat Willie. Dempsey reversed his loss. Then he put him in with Norton again. Dempsey flattened him in one round. His career then really took off. Apart from two other four round draws with Fat Willie, Dempsey decimated the heavyweight ranks. He took a special delight in taking out Fireman Jim Flynn in one round. Then Kearns got him a fight with Big Bill Brennan. Brennan was being groomed for a title shot. He had never been stopped and had over 40 knockouts to his credit. Dempsey's combination of speed and power crushed him in six rounds. In fact Dempsey hit him so hard, Brennan's ankle snapped. Many ringsiders were impressed enough to compare the newcomer with Bob Fitzsimmons.

A relatively poor showing against another great fighter, Billy Miske, actually prompted Willard to consider Dempsey as a suitable challenger. He bypassed his real chief challenger, Fred Fulton. Kearns was not found wanting. He set up a fight with Fulton. Dempsey then came into his own as a fighter. He blasted out Fulton in eighteen seconds, which included the referee's count. Now it was time for the champion to make his mind up. Two months later disaster struck. In what should have been an almost routine four round battle with Fat Willie Meehan, it all went wrong. All their previous four round bouts had been close enough. This fight was no exception. Possibly on the whim of some official, Fat Willie got the winners nod. Kearns had Dempsey back in the ring the next day with a stunning one round knockout over Jack Moran. Kearns then tried to convince the press that Fat Willie's victory was a fluke. In his next outing Fat Willie gave Kearns excuse some credibility. He lost a four round decision to Fred Fulton, who in turn wanted no further part of Dempsey. Kearns did not remain idle. He convinced the manager of the world's light heavyweight champion, Battling Levinsky, that Dempsey was just a club fighter. In short, a push over for a brilliant veteran like Levinsky. With 250 fights under his belt, he had never been stopped, nor was there a mark on him. He was and is regarded as an all time great. Dempsey stopped him in three rounds. Kearns then put him back in with Billy Miske. This time Dempsey redeemed himself. He almost caved Miske's ribs in, to win a unanimous decision. After a series of one round knock outs against some better than average opposition, Dempsey finally got his chance. The date was set for July 4th 1919 and Willard did not have the slightest inclination what he was letting himself in for.

Tex Rickard the promoter, whose name was to be indelibly linked with Dempsey and Kearns, at first, like Willard, thought Dempsey was too small and might even be killed. To reassure him, Kearns was kind enough to bet Rickard Dempsey's end of the purse, $10,000dollars, that the challenger would flatten Willard in one round. He did not bother telling Dempsey this until the last minute. Later, Rickard had other worries. He complained to Nat Fleischer, who was covering the fight, that the champion was not taking the fight seriously enough. He found him still in bed when he should have been out doing his roadwork. Willard simply repeated Rickard's earlier fears. ' He is too small. It will be over in a few rounds.' Yet Jess did put in some training, enough to last those three prophetic rounds.

Dempsey trained his heart out for nine hours a day. The brutal hardships of the hobo jungle were very much in his mind. He was also lucky enough to get the services of Jimmy de Forest one of the great trainers of the sport.

On a broiling hot day in Toledo Ohio, the fight was held in an open air arena. For all the pressure he was under, Dempsey at first circled the giant champion for about twenty seconds. Willard poked out a long left jab. Dempsey slipped under it then brought Willard crashing to the canvas with a devastating right hand to the jaw. For the first time in his career, albeit with an incredulous smile on his face, Willard sank to the canvas. He rose to his feet, but the challenger was on him like a tornado, punching from all angles. In those days a fighter was not obliged to go to a neutral corner in the event of a knock down. Dempsey constantly stood over him, determined to wrench the title at any cost. Six more times the giant crashed to the canvas, where he was finally counted out a sobbing wreck His hand was on the lower rope. His ribs and his cheek bone were broken, as was his nose and jaw, while his front teeth were scattered on the canvas. Dempsey quickly left the ring only to be frantically called back. The fight was not over yet. The noise of the crowd was such that no one heard the bell ring at the count of eight. Dempsey barely made it back as the second round began. He decided to coast until he got his second wind back. Willard lasted out the prophetic three rounds as the challenger still bided his time. Then it was all too much. Jess could not get off his stool to answer the bell for the fourth. It was over.

Willard was battered so badly, the question has often been asked if Dempsey's hand tapes had been dipped in plaster of Paris. The one person this angered almost as much as Dempsey was Nat Fleischer. He had been in Dempsey's dressing room and stood next to him while his hands were taped up. He swore that the only substance put on Dempsey's hands was water, when he complained about the heat. Willard's chief second was in the room and so was Daymon Runyon, sportswriter, author and world's champion cynic. Had he seen anything untoward, it would have been written up in large bold letters in his column that evening. The water may have had the effect of stiffening the tapes, but another fighter using the same tapes would not have had the same devastating effect. Dempsey himself felt he had not cheated. He took a great pride in his punching power, and was known to have stated reasonably,' What the hell did I need plaster of Paris for?'

Years later, when Kearns turned against him, he wrote an article in the prestigious Sports Illustrated Magazine, claiming that Dempsey's hand tapes had been dipped in plaster of Paris. Dempsey became so incensed at the slur, he went to a plaster of Paris manufacturers. They did a special test and declared that in order to have inflicted the kind of punishment he had done on Willard without hurting his own hands, the plaster of Paris would have to have been at least six inches thick. Fitzsimmons breaking his hands on Jefferies is a point in view.

What may have explained Willard's condition was that he took Dempsey too lightly. He carried three years ring rust, was 38 years old and in poor condition. Bringing all that into the ring against a lean, hungry Dempsey, he was lucky not to have been killed. For all that he was a human being, and Dempsey may have had some qualms of conscience. It apparently came out in his sleep that night. He dreamt their roles were reversed. It was Dempsey who took the vicious beating. So real was the dream that Jack got out of bed and looked in the mirror. He was unmarked, but still not convinced. He dressed and went out in the street. It was early morning and the papers had just hit the stands. He approached a newsboy. 'Hey kid,' he said. 'Who won the fight?' The kid scrutinised him. 'Ain't you Dempsey?' he demanded suspiciously. Dempsey sheepishly admitted he was. 'Well, you did, you fool,' snapped the kid.

Fat Willie Meehan's name was put forward for a first title defence, despite his loss to Fulton. Dempsey was quite happy about it. Meehan had stuck to him like glue in five four round fights. A ten or fifteen round battle would settle their differences once and for all. The fight fell through. Instead Billy Miske, desperate for money and having contacted Bright's disease, begged Dempsey for a match. Kearns, possibly thinking Miske the easier option, gave the go ahead. Miske would later knock out Fat Willie in one round.

Miske's illness had taken some edge off his performance, but it had far from debilitated him. Eye witnesses claim he looked in peak condition as he rounded off his training. As the fight began, Kearns thought so too. After two rounds he grumbled, 'He doesn't look that ill to me. Finish him.' When the bell sounded for the third round Dempsey dutifully opened up and dropped Billy for the full count.

Three months later Kearns accepted Bill Brennan as a challenger. Brennan had been Dempsey's means for breaking into the big time. Now he was back, putting his misfortunes behind him. He got into the shape of his life. By contrast, Dempsey was seen late at night, visiting the nightspots with Kearns He trained hard enough, but he clearly underestimated the challenger, and he paid a hard price for it. This was the first, but by no means the last time they would hand an advantage to a challenger. The result was that after ten hard fought rounds, the champion was trailing on points, and the title seemed to be slipping away. Kearns panicked accordingly. Somehow Dempsey dug deep down into himself, and with a fierce rally, battered the challenger senseless in the twelfth round. Brennan and Dempsey were good friends, and after the fight Brennan burst into Dempsey's dressing room and told the laughing champion, 'I'll get you next time.'

Kearns did not think it was so funny, yet he never seemed to have learned from it. For all that their next title defence broke all boundaries. It became the first million dollar gate. On July 22nd 1921 at Boyles thirty Acres in New Jersey Dempsey faced the new world's light heavyweight champion Georges Carpentier. Carpentier was not only another all time great, he was a war hero. This last was in contrast to the champion, who was hated for being an alleged slacker. A slacker being someone who was afraid to fight for his country. The slur was unjustified, but it was firmly believed. What sparked this off was a photograph taken of a young Dempsey, making his war effort as a welder in a dock yard. The young man was smiling, wearing overalls and patent leather shoes. When the war wounded began returning home, Dempsey became the most hated athlete in America. As Carpentier had been awarded the Croix de Guerre and the Medal Militaire many loyal Americans attended the fight in the hope of seeing Dempsey get his comeuppance. However, when Rickard got his first look at the Frenchman he panicked. Like some great fighters, George's looks were deceptive. He looked like a matinee idol. He had even been dubbed Gorgeous Georges and the Orchid Man. Yet he was a master craftsman with a deadly right hand that he threw with blinding speed. For all that, his slim build did nothing to allay Rickard's fears. He not only begged Dempsey not to knock him out in the first round, he begged him not to kill him. 'Even I could beat him,' he moaned. When the gross receipts of the gate were counted at $1,782,238 dollars, Rickard felt a little better. Dempsey easily took the first round. It was in the second round that the hopes of those who hated him were built up. Carpentier caught him with his vaunted right hand. It staggered the champion, but Carpentier came off worst, as the blow had broken his wrist and thumb. Carpentier complained in his autobiography that even when he did land a blow on the champion, it was like hitting a brick wall. Dempsey opened up in the fourth round, dropping the challenger for a nine count. Carpentier jumped up before the final second. Dempsey quickly moved in and caught him with a powerful blow to the jaw, and that was the end of it. The disappointment of the war veterans was lost in the uproar of the crowd. Meanwhile, the boys in the radio room reached a new level in international etiquette by signalling to a passing French ship, 'Your frog got flattened in the fourth.'

Rickard then jeopardised the Kearns Dempsey fortunes, when he was caught in bed with a young lady who was old enough to call him Daddy. He advised the dynamic duo to get lost for a while. They did. Hollywood called. The money kept rolling in and Jack became an actor. It was said he made some of the most forgettable movies of all time, but this might not have been fair, for they were quite popular. Two happy years crawled by, when it was possible that Kearns may have reminded himself that there was such a thing as ring rust.

He had been approached by the good people of Shelby, Montana. Encouraged by the gate receipts of the Carpentier fight, they offered Kearns £300,000dollars for Jack's services. His next defence would be in their fair city. Kearns demanded most of the money before the fight. With an effort, the citizens came up with it. However, it fell far short of the money taken at the gate. A mere 7,202 paying customers came through the turn styles. Moreover, Kearns didn't do Dempsey any favours in choosing Tommy Gibbons as a challenger. Gibbons was a great master, slightly past his best, but still more than useful. Dempsey, in contrast, was carrying two years ring rust. Although Kearns had the referee in his pocket, Dempsey did not need him. Gibbons took the first three rounds hands down, and then the champion got his act together. Over a 15 round time limit, he pounded out a 12-3 victory.

Both men complicated each other. Gibbons acknowledged Dempsey's mastery by stating that he knew all the tricks. Dempsey in turn said trying to hit Gibbons was like trying to thread a needle on a windy mountain top. Kearns demanded the rest of the money. Realising he was about to bust the town, he was alleged to have told Dempsey to let it go the distance in order to get their money, and make a quick getaway. Dempsey never admitted to such a thing, although he and Kearns bolted out of town as soon as the champion left the ring. One banker despaired that it was the greatest disaster to hit Montana since Custer's Last Stand.

As for Gibbons, he was paid nothing for his lumps. Rickard by this time was back in action, and he came up with a winner. From Argentina had come a huge fighter known as the 'Wild Bull of the Pampas.' He had conquered South America and now came north to seek to title. He was a ferocious fighter with a powerful punch and a tremendous ability to absorb a blow. He stood almost three inches taller than the champion and outweighed him by twenty pounds of solid muscle. He could also fight, having knocked out amongst others, Big Bill Brennan. Rickard could smell another million dollar gate, and he was right. The challenger was Luis Angel Firpo and if he had a weakness it was pure meanness, especially when it came to parting with money. Without realising or caring what he was doing, he threw away possibly his only chance by firing Dempsey's old trainer, Jimmy de Forest. He did this merely to save on training fees. He then hired the Olympic heavyweight champion as a sparring partner, because in those days Olympiads could not accept payment without losing their amateur status. During one sparring session the Olympic champion, miffed at Firpo's tight fistedness caught him against the ropes with his feet crossed. The temptation was too great. He moved in to finish him off when Firpo brought his great fist crashing down on the top of his head. The Olympiad said his head felt like a drawing pin being buried into a plank of wood.

The fight took place in the Polo Grounds in New York on September 14th 1923. Dempsey, Kearns and Rickard were back in business. The fans paid $1,188, 603 dollars to witness the brawl, for that is what it became. Shortly before the fight, the champion was given a strange request. Guarding his dressing room door was a tall, thick set marine. As a newspaperman showed him his pass to enter, the marine checked him, then said awkwardly,' Look….I've always wanted to know what it felt like to be knocked out by Dempsey…..Do you think he would oblige me?' The newspaperman gave him a strange look, and then nodded towards the door. 'Let's go in,' he said. Dempsey was lying on a table, covered with a towel with his eyes closed. 'Go ahead, 'said the newsman, 'Ask him.' Dempsey opened his eyes. All fighters, no matter how well they hide it, are nervous before a fight, and Dempsey had no time for fools. He listened grimly to this strange request, sat up, unloaded a lightening right hand to the marine's jaw, then lay back down on the table to continue his rest. The marine collapsed in a heap on the floor. A half an hour later, back on duty, he sported a swollen jaw that would proudly last him for weeks.

The bout is often referred to as the most exciting battle for the heavyweight crown of all time. How much ring rust Dempsey shed from the Gibbons fight is debatable. Firpo meanwhile, having got rid of de Forest, was totally unprepared for what he was about to receive. Within seconds of the first bell, he was flat on his back. He rose, determined to take the title and caught the champion with a powerful right to the jaw. Dempsey went down, crouching on the canvas, then sprang at him. Firpo crashed to the canvas six more times. Again, as the rules allowed, Dempsey stood over him. At times the challenger had to crawl on his hands and knees to give himself space to get to his feet. In a fury worthy of the wild bull he was named after, he got up to tear into his tormentor. He backed him up against the ropes, which were too slack, then suddenly the challenger found himself standing in the ring by himself. Dempsey had gone flying out of the ring to land hard on the reporters table. Flaying his arms wildly, he inadvertently gave a high court judge, who had used his influence to sit with the reporters, a monstrous black eye. He was desperately trying to get back in the ring within ten seconds, when the members of the press pushed him back inside. He might never have made it without them. De Forest would have been invaluable to Firpo at this point, and probably demanded a disqualification as the champion's re entry into the ring was not unaided. The members of the press defended their action however, claiming, 'Of course we pushed him back. What would you have done if a 192lb heavyweight came flying at you?' Some may consider that a reasonable argument. Once Dempsey was back on his feet, Firpo was too groggy to finish him off. Then the bell rang ending the first round. The second round lasted only 57 seconds. Firpo crashed to the canvas for the eighth time. He struggled up with a vague thought in his head. He saw an opening, or so the thought. He delivered a blow to Dempsey's side, and then attempted to follow it up with a powerful blow to the champion's jaw. Instead, Dempsey blocked Firpo's swing to his jaw, and turned it into a devastating left hook. It was finally too much. The game challenger was counted out.

The crowd exploded, although some wise sages thought the champion was beginning to slip. Yet the happiest of all was the high court judge. He showed his black eye to all and sundry exclaiming,' Look, Dempsey gave me that.'

Politics now came back into the heavyweight scene in the shape of the Afro American contender Harry Wills. He was deservedly Dempsey's chief challenger and Rickard's main headache. It churned up worries going back to 1910. The authorities never had to worry about Willard defending against a black challenger. This new champion seemed fit to have taken on Lil Artha in his prime, and he didn't care who he fought. Pressure had been put on Rickard, who in turn put pressure on Dempsey. Back in 1919 it had taken considerable arm twisting by Rickard to get Dempsey to state in the New York Times that he would not defend against a black fighter. This was embarrassing because Jack had just finished thanking Bill Tate for helping him prepare for Willard. Now it was 1923, and Dempsey made another statement to the press. He declared in the Wisconsin

Times that he welcomed the challenge from any black fighter. This may have been good news for Wills. Unfortunately, the authorities went back to worrying over potential race riots. The general theory, relating to those times, was that in the wake of Jack Johnson, the authorities put pressure on the promoters to never sanction a heavyweight title fight that included a black fighter, no matter how deserving. This theory was negated in part, when the great football player, actor, singer, and Civil Rights champion Paul Robeson, was offered large sums of money to fight Dempsey. Offers were made by promoters who for once, ignored the authorities. Kearns waited to see how much they would offer him for the champion's services. Finally it was Robeson who turned the whole thing down. He decided that boxing was not a suitable platform for the Civil Rights movement, and cited the negative influence of Jack Johnson.

Then a fight between Dempsey and Wills was agreed upon. Articles were signed and a date set for September 6th 1924 in Jersey City. The fight fell through, but for no fault of Dempsey. Then the champion was given the run around. The New York State Athletic Commission refused to sanction such a fight, again, for fear of race riots. They later stripped Dempsey of his licence to fight in New York for not meeting Wills. Rickard claimed he was warned off from putting on the fight by Governor Al Smith. James A.Farley, Chairman of the New York Commission denied this. Apparently Smith was not allowed to speak for himself. Some historians have ignored all this and put the blame solely on Dempsey, who in reality did not care who he fought. With all this bickering, Wills was left with nothing. Kearns took Dempsey back to Hollywood for more money spinning movies. Since the Firpo fight, Jack did not fight for three years. Wills went on to fight Firpo and won a close points decision.

By 1926 Rickard came up with another contender, and an all time great at that; Gene Tunney. Rickard wanted to put the fight on in New York. That was when the New York State Athletic Commission deprived Dempsey of his licence. It drove the proposed Tunney fight to Philadelphia. Rickard fixed the date for September 23. Dempsey had been living the high life for three years. He had a nose job to please the leading starlet of the day, Estelle Taylor. She thought he was the ugliest man she had ever seen, but she married him anyway. The great middleweight champion Mickey Walker was also managed by Kearns. He felt Kearns had been part of the rift that came between Dempsey and his young wife. Kearns felt he was entitled to a large percentage of everything Jack had, and according to Walker, he seemed to think that included Miss Taylor.

Dempsey was beginning to free himself from Kearns overbearing personality. There had been a blazing row over why he should not fight Harry Wills. The Southern Belle Miss Taylor took Kearns side, which did not help matters any. After three years Dempsey finally dumped Kearns and struck out on his own. It was now Dempsey and Rickard. Which meant Jack could keep all his end of the purse, rather than what Kearns decided to give him. Dempsey's biggest problem was shaking off three years ring rust. He was unable to do this with warm up fights. He had the impossible task in attempting it through training. He asked his pal Harry Greb to serve as his sparring partner, offering him a thousand dollars a round. Greb turned him down. 'Jack could never get in the kind of shape he needs to beat Tunney,' he said. He was right. In ten one sided rounds, the champion practically handed Tunney the title on a silver platter. Yet something happened to change Dempsey from a loathed and hated champion to an idolised legend. His wife approached him after the fight, and asked, 'What happened, Ginsberg?'

'Honey,' he replied,' I forgot to duck.' The fight crowd loved him for that. Jack's actual performance hardly warranted an immediate rematch. Yet to Kearns chagrin, it was another million dollar gate, and Rickard was not about to let Dempsey go. In fact he arranged for the ex champ to meet a powerful, exciting newcomer, Jack Sharkey. Sharkey had come to the fore by defeating the two leading black contenders. First George Godfrey, no relation to the original George Godfrey, then Wills himself. Only Dempsey stood in his way of a title match. They met in New York on July 21, 1927. It soon became clear that Dempsey was not the fighter he used to be. Sharkey stunned him in the first round and the ex champ struggled on into the seventh. Then his fortunes changed. He landed a controversial blow to Sharkey's mid section. There is still some doubt as to whether the blow was low or not. A photograph of the punch does not seem low. A clip from the film shows the blow does seem low. Gene Tunney, sitting at ringside, claimed the punch was not low. This might possibly imply that one cannot judge by fight films. Tunney added that it depended on where one was sitting. One might add, or the angle of the camera. If some of Dempsey's punches had been low, Sharkey may have felt enough was enough. But he forgot the oldest adage of the sport; namely, never take your eyes off your opponent. He also forgot who he was in there with. Consequently, he tried to grab Dempsey's arms, and turning to the referee cried,' Tell Dempsey to keep his ******* hands up.' All Dempsey could see was Sharkey's exposed chin. As he stated later, 'What was I supposed to do? Write him a letter?' Obviously a poor correspondent, Jack flattened him with a left hook instead. Over a million dollars had passed through the turn styles. Rickard happily signed the ex champ up for a rematch with Tunney.

On September 22 1927, the fans paid $2,658,660 dollars for one of the most controversial battles of all time, and they certainly got their money's worth. A new rule was introduced whereby in the event of a knock down, the fighter who scored it must go to a neutral corner before the count could begin. Neither fighter had any experience of this. The referee Dave Barry rigorously applied this rule, but only on Dempsey. He did not or would not, apply the rule to Tunney. The first half of the fight was almost a carbon copy of their first fight. Dempsey apparently got some of his old spark back and took the sixth round. In the seventh round he briefly got all of it back and knocked Tunney out. The problem was, obeying the new rule never entered his head. He refused to retreat to a neutral corner. Barry bravely frog marched him there, then returned to the stricken champion. Tunney by his own admission had no memory of this. He was still unconscious. The time keeper, seeing Barry in the counting position, called out,' FIVE.' Barry ignored him, and allowed Gene an extra second. At the time keeper's count of six Barry called out, 'ONE.' Gene could still not hear him He claimed he first heard

Tunney and the referee independently strive to keep the atmosphere as Tunney friendly as possible

the count of two, seven by the time keeper's count. He said later that he could have got up any time after the count of five. Lining this up with the time keeper's count, it was another way of saying that he could have got up after he count of ten. Some eyewitnesses disagreed, and accused Barry of slowing the count down. The legendary featherweight Abe Attell docked Gene's visit to the canvas with a stop watch at 22 seconds. Other stop watch claimants recorded 16 and 20 seconds. The controversy will no doubt continue. Gene got up at the referee's count of 9, and landed a murderous punch under Dempsey's heart. Dempsey thought he was going to die. He was not alone. Five men did die from heart attacks, listening to the fight over the radio. To even the score, Tunney knocked Dempsey down in the eighth round, and it also never entered Gene's head to retreat to a neutral corner. Barry quickly rushed in to start the count leaving Tunney hovering close by. He clearly made no attempt to send the champion anywhere. As it was, Dempsey quickly jumped up. Gene jumped back on his bicycle, to dominate the rest of the fight and retain the title. Dempsey refused a third fight with Tunney for fear of losing his eyesight. He lingered on in the sport, fighting exhibitions, but he never engaged in another professional fight. Despite his age, he enlisted in the Second World War, to clear the lingering slur of being a slacker. He saw action in the Pacific and was said to have captured a Japanese soldier with his bare hands. He became a legend in his own lifetime. The Wall Street crash wiped him out as it had millions of others. He refereed both boxing and wrestling matches. He even defeated some well known wrestlers in mixed matches. He appeared in movies, was a welcome honoured guest at many function, and fronted for a restaurant that became world famous. Many a fighter, black and white, had reason to be grateful for his generosity. For many of those who were fortunate enough to have seen him fight, he was always remembered as 'The Champ'.

Gene Tunney
The fighting Marine

The Fighting Marine

Gene Tunney, despite his clean cut college boy looks, came from a working class background, and was a product of the streets of New York. As a boy, he had his share of street fighting. He showed a natural aptitude for boxing. At his peak he was sometimes compared to James J. Corbett as a scientific fighter. Gene's greatest fights were really as a light heavyweight. He cut his teeth on such immortals as Harry Greb, Tommy Loughran and Battling Levinsky. In World War One he joined the American Expeditionary Forces. He won the light heavyweight title in France. Although he never saw action in the war, later, on winning the heavyweight crown, he was made an honorary colonel.

What really moulded Gene into such a formidable fighter, were his four bouts with that human threshing machine Harry Greb. Gene thought he was heading towards a world title when he defeated Battling Levinsky for the American light heavyweight title. He put that title on the line against Greb and received the only loss on his record. He also received such a beating that he collapsed in his dressing room. He never lacked a champion's courage, demanded a rematch, but had to take his place in line. Greb's prowess were so great that first he successfully defended his newly won title against Tommy Loughran. Then came his defence against Tunney. Gene was lucky enough to have attracted the attention of the immortal Benny Leonard, who gave him invaluable advice. It helped him take his title back, admittedly by the narrowest of margins. They were to fight on two more occasions before Greb finally had enough of him. Gene took a narrow decision over Tommy Loughran, and then concentrated on the heavyweights. He stopped the former world's light heavyweight champion Georges Carpentier in fourteen rounds. He next stopped another aging all time great, Tommy Gibbons. It was Gibbons only stoppage in a long career. Next came an important win over 'Rubber Man' Johnny Risko. At this point Tex Rickard was impressed enough to match him with Dempsey, who had finally returned to the ring wars. At the Sesquicentennial Stadium of Philadelphia Tunney took the heavyweight title in a very one sided affaire. A year later he won the controversial 'Battle of the Long Count'. Both fights, admittedly thanks to Dempsey, were million dollar gates. Gene had become a very rich young man.

In his own way, Tunney followed the old masters and tried to change his life style. And like them, he used the prestige of being the heavyweight champion of the world.

He tried to 'better' himself by getting into high society. He even managed to befriend the irascible playwright and wit, George Bernard Shaw. In fact, for different reasons, they used each other. Gene seemed to have been a rather pretentious young man. Sitting next to Shaw at a dinner function, he deliberately placed a copy of one of Shakespeare's plays on the table. Possibly to show he was capable of discussing such a book. No one took up the challenge. Gene had yet to learn that most of the 'smart set' do not actually read Shakespeare. They attend his plays in order to be seen by other 'smart setters', who also go to be seen. Yet Tunney and Shaw did cultivate each other. In fact Shaw wrote a book on the fight game. He recorded his meeting and admiration for James J. Corbett. He also wrote on the 'Battle of the Long Count.' Shaw, like all great writers, was in love with words, but in writing of the fight he seemed to be suffering from verbal diarrhoea. He could not stop himself from waxing eloquent to the point where the reader completely looses the plot of what he was trying of say. As Oscar Wilde once quipped of him,' He has no enemies and even his friends don't like him.'

However, before plunging into the smart set, Gene planned one last title defence. Many thought his challenger should have been Jack Sharkey. And in all fairness Rickard did give him a chance. The only other challenger at that time was the rugged New Zealander Tom Heeney. Rickard set up the fight, but it was not one of Sharkey's good nights. He could get no better than a draw. And as he had already lost to Dempsey, Heeny got the chance.

On July23 1928, in the Yankee Stadium Gene looked devastating in stopping the challenger in eleven one sided rounds. He now felt it time to call it quits. The fight itself was a financial loss for Rickard. He was $150,000 dollars out of pocket. Like it or not, the great thing missing in his life was Dempsey. Great as Tunney was, there was no one to match Dempsey's colour, excitement and drawing power. Gene may have resented this, but he was completely unmarked, rich and happy to announce his retirement. He was also happy to announce his engagement to Miss Polly Lauder, the cream of high society and an heiress to boot. To completer his success story he proved to be an astute businessman.

Tunney was one of the great technicians of the sport. He had a stiff punch and a brilliant left jab. Few fighters have equalled that jab, none have ever surpassed it. For some reason, the fans never took him to their hearts and many historians have underestimated him. Perhaps like Corbett and Ezzard Charles, he defeated a legend. Yet he should be remembered for the supreme craftsman and great fighter that he was.

Max Schmeling
An ambitious man who never gave up

The Caretaker Champions.

With Tunney's retirement, there was a vacuum that lasted two years. The promoters admitted they yearned for another Dempsey. In 1930, they at least found one who looked like him. This was the German, Max Schmeling. He proved to be a gifted light heavyweight, but with a slightly spotted record. On coming to America, he changed managers and his fortunes greatly improved. His new manager was Joe Jacobs, otherwise known as Yussel the Muscle. Having grown into a heavyweight, Max was guided towards a title fight with Jack Sharkey, who still had designs on the crown. Sharkey blasted his way back into contention with a stunning victory over the great Tommy Loughran, via a three round knockout. That followed a foul ridden victory over England's Phil Scott. Apparently, it was Sharkey who did all the fouling. Schmeling was on a collision course with him, by knocking out the highly rated Johnny Risko, the 'Rubber Man'. This was followed by another impressive win over the Basque Fascist Paulino Uzcudun.

The eventual showdown for the title took place on June 11, 1930, at the Yankee Stadium. Many experts have thought that this could have been the last of Sharkey's great fights. It seemed he could not be contained. He took command of the fight with a show of great speed and power. He battered the German to completely dominate the first three rounds. The pounding continued into the fourth, when Sharkey threw it all away by burying his glove in Schmeling's groin. Max collapsed to the canvas in agony. The referee started to count him out. Despite the pain, Schmeling started to get up. Yussel

Jack Sharkey
A great but temperamental fighter who threw
away two of his greatest chances

screamed at him to stay down. With great trust, Max obeyed his manager. Help was on its way. Arthur Brisbane, the editor of the powerful Hearst Publications, threatened the referee, telling him if he did not disqualify Sharkey, he would have the Walker Law repealed. The problem was, the referee did not see the low blow, and neither did one of the judges. The other judge did see it, and the threat to boxing was real enough. Consequently, for the first and last time, the heavyweight title was won on a foul. Yet a bad feeling flowed through the boxing world. Sharkey, known as a notorious fouler anyway, was in disgrace. For Schmeling it was even worse. He became a laughing stock, even in Germany. Yet for all that, he was recognised as the undisputed heavyweight champion of the world.

To his credit, he set out to prove it. On July 3rd, 1931, in Cleveland Ohio, the champion looked brilliant in a hard fought battle, to stop the great Young Stribling in the closing minutes of the fight. Sharkey also fought his way back to prominence. He won a crisp points victory over a onetime circus strong man, Primo Carnera. This created a public demand for a final showdown between Schmeling and Sharkey. On June 21, 1932 in Long Island New York, Schmeling convinced everyone but the referee that he was the real champion. Many in the fight crowd were angered, as Gunboat Smith, acting as third man, raised Sharkey's hand as the winner and new champion. Schmeling's volatile manager Yussel the Muscle aired his protest and dented the English language by screaming,' We wuz robbed. We shoulda stood in bed.' Both men had fought a cautious fight, relying mostly on left jabs. They went out of their way to avoid any fouls. It was not an exciting fight. And certainly nothing compared to what their first fight might have been. For all that, most people thought the German had done more than enough to win. Paradoxically, Schmeling once again became a hero. His dignity was restored, especially back in Germany. As for Sharkey, he showed nothing of the great fighter he had been in the 1920s. Since his victory over Carnera had earned him a chance at the title, he felt he had an easy defence in giving Primo a chance. The fight aroused more curiosity than amazement, when the light hitting giant stopped Sharkey in six rounds. Even today, many historians feel the fight was a tank job. Yet despite a sceptical world, including Sharkey's sceptical wife, Jack always denied it. Sharkey even sang Carnera's praises, stating the Italian was a much better fighter than people gave him credit for. There is little doubt that many, if not most Carnera's victories were fakes. His real earning potential was based on his great size, and fierce looking appearance. He was enormously strong, but a weak hitter. Primo had been discovered by Leon See, working as a circus strong man. See brought him over to America where his contract was 'taken over' by some odious characters. These gentlemen were aligned to the notorious gangster Owny Madden. Primo won a series of suspicious knock outs, which the naïve Italian believed were real. Yet his points losses to top liners like Larry Gains and Jack Sharkey, at least show he was proficient enough to go the distance with world class performers. What really boosted his stock was his bout with Ernie Shaaf. Shaaf was a gifted, hard hitting fighter, who had been badly hurt by the murderous punches of newcomer Max Baer.

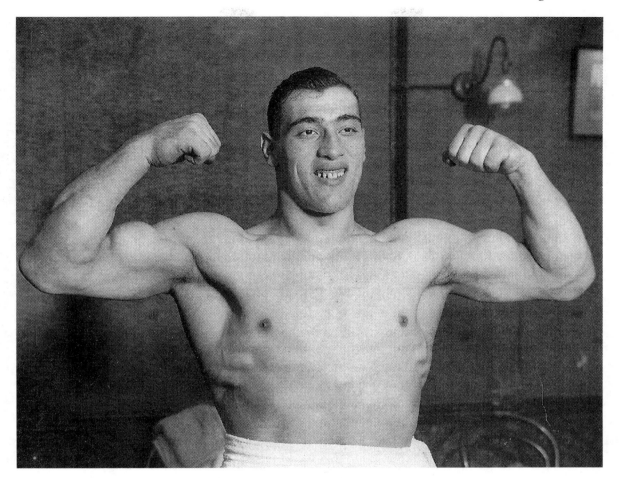

Primo Carnera. Little Satchel Feet.
He had a wrestler's strength, but was a weak hitter.

Although he went on to win a couple of fights, it was in his fight with Carnera that Shaaf went down from a relatively light tap. He was counted out and died from head injuries a few days later. Primo's 'brains trust', showing no remorse, were quick to point out what a devastating puncher the Italian giant really was. It was strongly believed that Shaaf died from a delayed reaction from his fight with Baer. Max certainly believed it. It was to haunt him for the rest of his life.

Now Primo was champion he did show some ability. He out pointed the experienced Paulino Uzcudun. Next he won over aging all time great Tommy Loughran. Carnera enjoyed a weight advantage of 86lbs. The old master did take some unusual precautions. He smeared his hair with foul smelling fish oil that often kept Primo at bay. Carnera used his tremendous weight advantage by stepping on Loughran's feet, to the point of breaking some of his toes. He found it impossible to knock out the elusive veteran, and retained the title on a points win. Then the honeymoon was over. Primo's next title defence was against Shaaf's' real conqueror, Max Baer. Baer utterly destroyed him.

Baer possessed an unlimited talent that he never developed. He was certainly one of the most lethal punchers in the history of the game. Unfortunately, he never took anything seriously, including , if not especially, himself. He earned a title shot with a surprising knock out win over Max Schmeling. He came from behind, seemingly on his way to a points loss when he devastated the German with his overwhelming punching power.

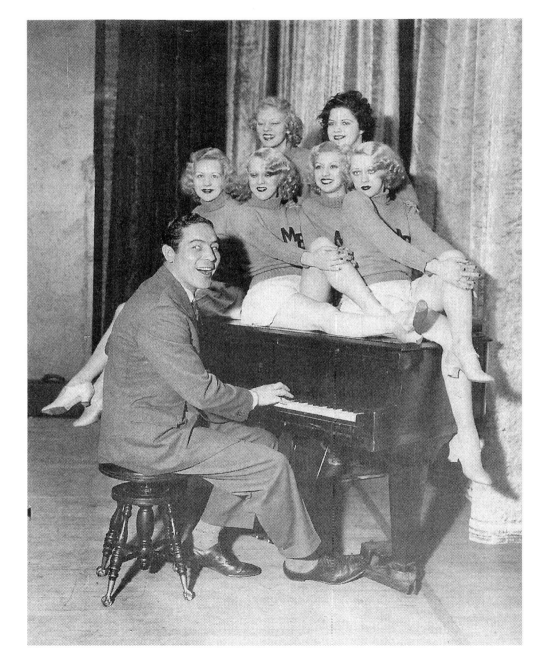

Max Bear
Champion Max with everything under control

The title fight against Carnera took place at the Garden Bowl, in Long Island, New York on June 14th 1934. It became known as the comedy battle and the nick names the sportswriters and fans bestowed on the combatants said it all. The 6ft 5 and a half inch Canera was known affectionately as 'Little Satchel Feet' and the 'Ambling Alp' while Baer was known appropriately as 'Madcap Maxie', 'The Clown Prince', and Max's own favourite, 'The Beautiful Building With The Weak Roof.' And if anyone thought this battle took all the dignity out of the heavyweight championship of the world, they would be right. Carnera admittedly showed all the raw courage of a champion, but his bravery was often lost in a welt of laughter. Baer knocked him to

Carnera goes down v Max Baer (right)

the canvas eleven times. The challenger toyed with the champion. At one point he dropped to the canvas with him, 'Just to keep him company' and crying out,' Last's one up is a sissy.' The referee did not think it was so funny, and stopped the slaughter in the eleventh round. For all that the fans and sportswriters thought Baer would retain the title for at least ten years.

Since Dempsey and then Tunney's early retirement, the fans had been disappointed. Schmeling, a great fighter though he was, had won the title on a foul, and then lost it in a fight most thought he had won. Sharkey, not the fighter he was, won that dubious decision, and lost the title in far more dubious circumstances. Baer at last, seemed the real thing, but hardly one to put dignity back in the sport. As for Schmeling, his fortunes were at low ebb and along with Sharkey, he became one of boxing's forgotten men.

Carnera's 'associates' had still not finished with him. There was still meat to be plucked from his bones. The prestige of being an ex world's champion still meant something. Squeezing one last payday out from him they threw him in with the legendary Joe Louis. Joe decimated him in six rounds. Primo was said to have returned to Italy, flat broke on a cattle boat. After the war he returned to America, where he excelled in the profession he was born for; wrestling. Allowing that many grappling matches were entertaining fakes, this was by no means true of all bouts. Primo held the great Frank Sexton to a draw in a title match. He also had the satisfaction of a rematch with Larry Gains. Gains, was down on his luck, and like many ex fighters, resorted to wrestling. Primo was no sentimentalist, and he did have a long memory. After their bout Larry was carried from the ring and taken to hospital. Primo was to die a rich and successful man. And in spite of what Jack Sharkey's wife thought, believed he was once the undisputed heavyweight champion of the world.

Baer was to disappoint a lot of people in never realising his great potential. He was hardly ever in good shape, for most part relying on his devastating right hand. It is often said he could have been ranked among the all time greats, and he had every opportunity to do so. Dempsey himself encouraged him, and even trained him for some of his important fights. His victories over Tom Heeney, Kingfish Levinsky and Schmeling, put him in line for a chance at the title. Tragically, on his climb to the championship, he was responsible for the deaths of two men. This was to torment him to the end of his life.

Prior to meeting Carnera, Max starred in a leading role with the lovely Myna Loy, in a movie called 'The Prize-fighter and the Lady.' Carnera himself played a small but significant role. He also fell victim to Baer's sense of humour. As they were signed up to fight, it was only natural that Baer would try to psyche him. Of all the pranks he played, the worst was when he electrocuted the Primo's chair. The film crew were amazed to see the fuming champion chasing the challenger and leading man around the movie lot. Max would have been better off staying in the movies. Unlike most fighters who turned to acting, he really did have charisma and talent. Yet his first and only title defence might possibly have robbed him of that.

Boxing has produced many rags to riches stories, but Jimmy Braddock's would be hard to beat. He seemed to have been something of a fighter who could look bad against bad fighters, yet could hold his own against good fighters. When it really counted, he could hold his own against some great ones. He began as a light heavyweight with a good knockout record. He lost handily in his first title bid against the great Tommy Loughran. He gradually faded out of the picture, plagued too often, like so many fighters, with hand trouble. Fights were suddenly hard to come by. The Great Depression hit almost everyone, and Braddock, with a family to feed ended up as a longshoreman, then finally on relief.

Jimmy Braddock, The Cinderella Man
One of the greatest rags to riches story ever

The rags to riches story began when a promising young fighter named Corn Griffin needed a name, but not too dangerous a fighter, to boost his record. Someone came up with the name James J. Braddock. Jimmy fit the bill perfectly. He had grown into a heavyweight, and had once fought for a world title; moreover, he was ring rusty. Yet he also desperately needed to fill the family coal bin and put food on the table. He went on to annoy some very important people by flattening Griffin in three rounds. The reason these important people were upset, was because they could not see Braddock as championship material, so they tried to get rid of him. The great John Henry Lewis was chosen to do the job. Lewis had once held a victory over him, and was prepared to do it again. On the night in question, John Henry picked himself up off the canvas to lose a close, but clear decision. Braddock next appeared on the under card of the Carnera Baer fight. His opponent was Art Lasky, a tough fighter who was now being groomed for a title shot. After fifteen hard fought rounds, Braddock's hand was raised as the winner. He was now the chief challenger to Baer's newly won crown.

It is possible that Damon Runyon's coining Braddock the 'Cinderella Man', may have in part, and contributed to Baer's downfall. Most people in the public eye have a deep seated need to be popular. And suddenly the very popular Baer was cast as the 'bad guy.' On June13 1935, Max defended the title in the same ring, he had won it. The clowning went on. This time the fighter in the opposite corner was an experienced craftsman who had no time for foolishness. Before the fight Baer's behaviour was very strange, even for him. He invited a prostitute into his dressing room in order to take his mind off the fight. In those days, as today, there is a belief in the fight game, that sex weakens a fighter. Max however; put all his faith in the power of his right hand.

When the fight started, to the astonishment of the crowd and the chagrin of his corner men, Max clowned his way through the fight. It was as though he was in a world of his own. In the fading rounds he actually did land his vaunted right hand. Against all odds, Braddock stood up to the blow, and shook it off. Baer never had the chance to land another one. In the end he was trying too hard. At the final bell, the championship was no longer his.

Baer more recently, received another burst of fame from the movie, 'The Cinderella Man. ' It is doubtful if the scriptwriter, or the director, Ron Howard, had any respect for the fight game, or knew or cared who Max Bear was. With mindless insensitivity, they created a black and white, hero villain scenario. Bear was portrayed as a heartless monster, who boasted and delighted in taking the lives of Campbell and Shaaf. Nothing could have been further from the truth. Had the unimaginative script writer and director developed Baer's character more true to life, they might have come up with an all time classic. It was a movie that should have paid homage to two great fighters with two very different personalities. That was their loss.

Baer's defeat was considered one of the major upsets of the game. And his career slowly went into decline. He played small parts in movies, especially after his retirement as a fighter. But he was never again in demand as a leading man. His movie with Myna Loy was a one off. A year after losing the title he became cannon fodder for the up and coming Joe Louis. It may have been the worst night of his career. Dempsey got Baer in the best of condition, and was in his corner. A reporter stopped Louis on his way to the ring and asked him, 'Does Dempsey being in Baer's corner bother you, Joe?'

'Can he hit me from there?' asked Joe dryly.

'Well no,' replied the reporter.

'Then he don't bother me' said Joe. That just about said it all. Yet Baer was bothered enough. There is a symptom many fighters get when their hands feel so brittle, that the pain becomes unbearable to the slightest touch. Braddock suffered often from this in his career. Of all nights, it happened to Baer. He was given an injection to kill the pain. Unfortunately, the fight was postponed because of rain. By the time the fighters were called to the ringside to effects of the injection had worn off. It was dangerous to give him another shot. Baer never lacked courage, but under the circumstances, he tried to have the fight called off. Over Baer's protests, Dempsey apparently bullied him to go through with it. Max took a terrible beating that night. He gamely got up after the first knockdown, but on going down again, he decided enough was enough. Despite some criticism from people who did not know what it felt to be hit by Joe Louis, Max stayed down .Some thought he could have got up. Baer quipped it was going to cost more than $50 dollars a ringside seat to see him get killed. He nevertheless continued fighting. He looked impressive in knocking out Two Ton Tony Galento, and even indirectly embarrassed Louis. After Joe won the title, his first title defence was against the rugged Welshman Tommy Farr. The fight went the whole rout, with both fighters slugging it out at the final bell. There had been no knock downs. Later, for some reason, Baer again got himself into the shape of his life, and also took on the Welshman. Baer had him down twice and won a clear 15 round decision. Max's last fight was in 1941 against Lou Nova. Baer was on the wrong end of a bad beating when he caught Nova a devastating blow. He could have finished him off. Instead, he backed away and let him recover, although it meant losing the fight. Perhaps he did not want another death on his conscious. The makers of 'The Cinderella Man' movie have a lot to answer for.

With the title changing hands often, Schmeling, while considered a thing of the past, was still active and still ambitious. The one thing that had kept him going was the memory of a sparring session he had had in his youth with Dempsey in Germany. Dempsey had been so impressed with the youngster, he predicted he would one day become a world champion. He achieved that dream, but without the dignity that supposedly went with the job. He was truly a great fighter, but it seemed the whole thing had slipped through his fingers. After his loss to Sharkey, Schmeling bounced back with a win over Mickey Walker, and then he was stopped by Baer. This followed another loss to Steve Hamas. His career now seemed definitely over. He suddenly sprang back with a win over Walter Neusal, and then scored a revenge knock out over Hamas. He went on to stop Paulino Uzcudun in 12 rounds. Politics then took over his life. Worst of all, he became identified with Adolph Hitler and the Third Reich. Paradoxically, he was still managed by the intrepid Joe 'Yussel the Muscle' Jacobs, who was Jewish. Hitler was known to have raised a questioning eyebrow over this, but Schmeling stood his ground. He explained that he needed Jacobs if he were ever to regain the heavyweight title. Hitler accepted this as he wanted Germany to have the crown to support his master race theories. It became Schmeling's misfortune to be identified with that.

Max was an intelligent, strong minded man, but he was also very ambitious. To the best of his ability he used the Reich, as much as it used him. This relationship was very short lived, but for a while he became Hitler's blue eyed boy and it was a long time before he was able lived it down.

The uncertainties of the fight game now took an even more extreme turn. Coming out of Detroit was a young fighter who was already being compared with other Afro American heroes like Jack Johnson and Sam Langford. He was one of the fight game's super greats; Joe Louis. Joe had destroyed Primo Carnera in six rounds, and then finished Max Baer in four. His handlers were then offered a title fight with Braddock. Jack Johnson's jinx seemed to have been broken at last. Yet after careful consideration, Joe's brain trust felt he needed just one more warm up fight, preferably against another former champion. They chose Schmeling. Some cynics thought the German would be killed. Schmeling had other ideas. He obtained films of Joe's most recent fights, which he played over and over again, looking for some kind of weakness. Then he saw something Joe did over and over again. He tended to drop his left hand, as he came over to deliver his devastating right. This left him open to a right hand counter punch, and Schmeling packed dynamite in his right hand.

Max then got support from an unexpected source; Jack Johnson. Johnson was always critical of what he saw as Joe's lack of balance. He predicted that a fast clever heavyweight with a stiff punch could knock him out. He went on to predict that Schmeling was that man. He went so far as to put his money where his mouth was, and bet heavily on the German to win.

The fight took June 19th 1936 in the Yankee Stadium. As Joe remembered it in his autobiography, Schmeling almost broke his jaw in the second round, knocked him down in the fourth, then after a heroic struggle, knocked him out in the twelfth. Max, to the horror of the American government, was now Braddock's official chief challenger. Certainly few gave Braddock much of a chance against him. Yet ominously for Max's chances, he was once again the darling of Germany. Only this time it was Nazi Germany. Hitler himself, personally exclaimed Schmeling was his favourite fighter. This practically decimated Max's chances of getting a championship fight. Schmeling of course, was no Nazi, and never believed in Hitler's half baked racial theories. Unfortunately, on both sides of the Atlantic, no one seemed to care what Schmeling thought.

Hitler used Schmeling to persuade the Americans to send their athletes to the 1936 Olympic Games, to be held in Berlin. His main job was to convince them that Germany's treatment of the Jews was greatly exaggerated. Although he succeeded in this, it was hardly his finest hour. However, as stated, he was an ambitious man, and his title chances depended on the mutual goodwill between America and Germany. Ironically, Yussel the Muscle, Max's Jewish manager, was right in the middle of all this. There was an infamous picture taken of Yussel at a Nazi gathering, with a sheepish grin on his face, giving the Nazi salute with a cigar stuck between his fingers. The picture shocked and infuriated those back home. And opinions were divided. The bartenders in the places Yussel used to frequent in New York swore they would slip a Mickey Finn in his drinks. Others simply wanted to string him up from the nearest lamppost. Yussel assured everyone that while it was true, he did give the Nazi salute, his other hand was behind his back and his fingers were crossed, so it didn't count. Adolph's opinion on all this was never recorded, although it was said to have coincided with the first time he got on his hands and knees and started chewing up the carpet. For all the hype, in practical terms, Schmeling's fight with Braddock was boycotted. The light now shone on the greatest fighter since Dempsey and Tunney.

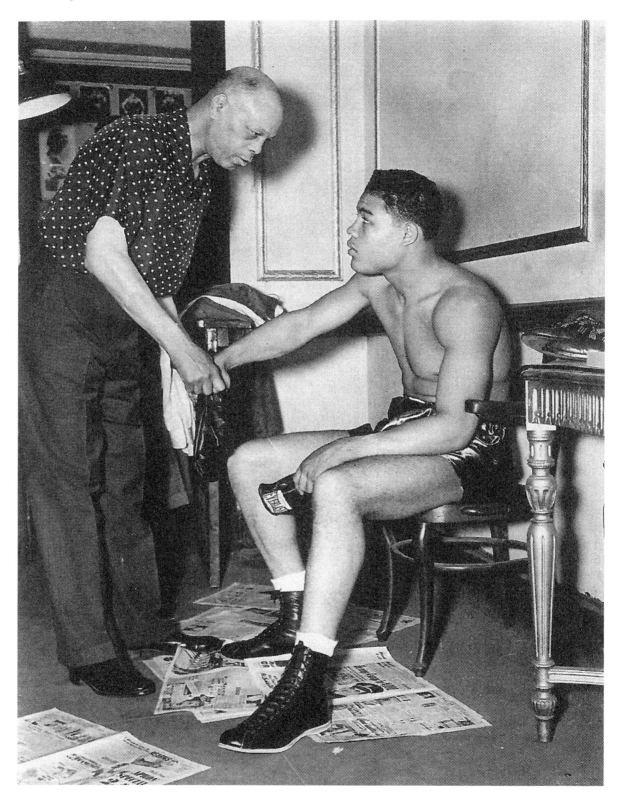

Joe Louis and Jack Blackburn
The fighter trainer relationship has rarely been equalled

The Brown Bomber

J oe Louis in a sense was one of the first package fighters. He was on the top of the bill from his first fight to his last. He was brought along with care. Although he was never fed the dead bodies to pad his record, like so many modern fighters. Joe's mother thought her son had beautiful hands, and entertained the thought that one day he might become a violinist. She bought him a violin and gave him money for his weekly lessons. Joe dutifully went along, but he was not sure if this was his true vocation. He had more than just a hankering to attend Brewster's gym. One day a neighbourhood kid settled it for him. He made fun of Joe and his violin. Joe's response was to break the violin over the kid's head. His music fees consequently ended up in the pocket of the trainer at Brewster's. Joe never actually got around to telling his mother. She believed her baby her was still practicing his scales. One day the trainer threw him in with a more experienced boy. He was an amateur champion. Joe took an awful beating. He might have hidden the fact that his violin was no more. The bruises on his face were another matter. With little choice, he came clean. His mother hid her disappointment, and gave him her blessing.

Joe developed into a brilliant amateur. His tremendous punching power attracted the attention of two small time racketeers, John Roxborough and Julian Black. They in turn persuaded the legendary Jack Blackburn to handle him. It needed a lot of persuading. Blackburn was of the same generation as Jack Johnson and Sam Langford, who had fought him. He firmly believed that no black fighter would ever get the chance to compete for the heavyweight title. Perhaps there was something about Joe that made him change his mind. Blackburn was an ex jail bird who had become a hard drinking cynic. Ironically, they developed a father son relationship, and over the years it formed the basis of Joe developing into a near perfect fighting machine. As an amateur Joe won the light heavyweight championship of America. He soon grew into a heavyweight and joined the paid ranks. At first his professional opponents were carefully chosen, but they were hardly soft touches. He soon graduated into knocking out top notch fighters. The more than useful Stanley Poreda, Natie Brown and Hans Birkie were among his knockout victims. As Joe's name became better known he attracted some friendly support from an unexpected source.

A magazine editor noticed the similarity between Joe's name, and that of the famous night club entertainer Joe E. Lewis. He thought it might boost Joe's career if they had their picture taken together. The great comedian, something of a fight fan, said he was glad to oblige. A morning session was arranged, with Lewis's agent, but not with Lewis. The problem was Lewis never got to bed before three in the morning. Trying to wake him before three in the afternoon was a non event. Joe and the photographer turned up at the door at 11a.m. Neither ringing on the bell nor pounding on the door drew any results. Finally, they gave up. When Lewis was later reminded of his promise, he dismissed the whole thing and curtly responded, 'Ah, I bet the kid's no good anyway.' When assured the 'kid' was very good, Lewis perversely replied that he would bet against him in all his fights, and probably reap a fortune. This bad judgement proved to be a costly business as Joe went on to cut down Carnera, Baer and Uzcudun. In Joe's first fight with Schmeling, Lewis was about to place a large bet on the German. Al Jolson stopped him. 'How can you bet on that Nazi b------?' he demanded. Lewis relented. For the first time he bet heavily on Joe. When Schmeling won by a twelfth round knockout, Lewis never spoke to Jolson for six months.

Up to that point, Joe had seemed unstoppable. And despite his youth, he took his defeat philosophically. Two months later he was back in the ring against Schmeling's one time conqueror, Jack Sharkey. The ex champion was now thirty six and over the hill. He was really lured back to fight Joe as a confidence booster. Sharkey was stopped inside three rounds. He now enjoyed the dubious honour of having been flattened by both Dempsey and Louis.

Joe's comeback trail was impressive. He went on a knockout spree of all the leading contenders. Only the great light heavyweight Bob Pastor broke Joe's K.O. run, which he did by largely back peddling. A rematch with Natie Brown ended in another knock out. Then just a year after his sole defeat, Joe found himself matched with Braddock for the title.

One might ask, what had happened to Schmeling? The Garden Corporation had an agreement for Schmeling to fight Braddock for the title. Mike Jacobs, a protégée of Tex Rickard, who owned the Twentieth Century Club, made the champion a better bid. He offered Jimmy 10% of all the heavyweight title fights for the next ten years, plus a large sum for defending against Louis. Added to which, given Hitler's treatment of the Jews in Europe, the Jewish lobby in America tried to boycott any title fight that involved Schmeling. Most people felt that had Braddock defended against Schmeling, his legitimate chief challenger, the title certainly would have gone to Nazi Germany. So Braddock accepted Jacob's lucrative offer. Schmeling was left out in the cold, and he was hardly in a position to explain that while he was Hitler's favourite fighter, that did not necessarily mean Hitler was Max's favourite lunatic. Braddock had not fought since he took the title from Baer two years before. His loss to Louis was considered a foregone conclusion. Jimmy did not see it that way. In Chicago on June 22nd 1937, the fight had hardly begun when the challenger found himself dumped on the canvas. Joe rose quickly to systematically tear the champion apart. Braddock simply would not give up. He went out after eight one sided rounds. Joe always affectionately referred to Braddock as 'The Champ', and called him the gamest fighter he ever met.

Now the stigma of Jack Johnson was broken, along with a very large dent in the colour bar. Joe was one of the most beloved of champions. Children the world over, regardless of race, creed or colour, wanted to be like him. Despite the brutality of his profession, he became the ideal role model. He was loved by everyone. Perhaps not by white racist America or the kid he had beaned with his violin, but certainly just about everybody else. Yet in all the euphoria, Schmeling was not as forgotten as may be assumed. Joe remembered him, and he wanted his revenge. For while Max was still active, and still the chief challenger, Joe never felt he was really the champion. Nevertheless, Joe's brain trust did not want to take any unnecessary chances. They decided to keep Max waiting for at least another year. Time was on their side, not Schmeling's. Yet aware of the dangers of ring rust, he knew he must get himself in some kind of shape. So eighteen months after he had beaten Louis, he fought again in America. He knocked out Harry Thomas in eight rounds. Then he engaged in two more warm up fights, and was then offered a title fight with Louis. Joe also fought Harry Thomas, and clipped three rounds off Schmeling's feat by knocking him out in five.

Joe was now at his absolute peak, and few gave the German much of a chance. The champion seemed to enjoy every advantage. He was younger; two years more experienced, and held a psychological advantage in that Schmeling was seen as a symbol of evil. With Hitler behind him and Joe Louis in front of him, Max may have briefly wondered if it was all worth it. Yet his ambition was such that he obviously did.

The fight took place on June 22nd 1938. 70,000 fans paid out for a million dollar gate to view the spectacle. Schmeling was greeted with boos and hisses on his way to the ring. Some even pelted him with banana skins. Ironically, in that entire crowd, Max only had about two known supporters, and they were both Jewish. His loyal manager Yussel the Muscle, and the ever green Joe E. Lewis. Despite more protests from Jolson, Lewis had placed a large bet on Schmeling, still hoping to recoup his losses.He certainly picked the wrong night for it. The atmosphere was so electric and hostile to the challenger, that one might wonder if Schmeling had landed that million to one shot and knocked Joe out again, would he have got out of the stadium alive? Max did almost lose his life, but it was entirely at the hands of the champion. He was brave enough, but almost helpless before Joe's onslaught. Schmeling was down almost as soon as the round began. He gamely rose to be knocked down again. As he rose Joe was on him, pounding him with deadly accurate punches. Max twisted his body as Joe drove pile driving blows into his back breaking a vertebra. Schmeling's chief second threw in the towel. The referee threw it out again. As the timekeeper reached the count of eight, the referee Arthur Donovan halted the fight. Joe's revenge was complete. The fight had been broadcast over Germany, but it was quickly cut off the air. At least, if nothing else, Max was finally relieved of the 'honour' of being Hitler's favourite fighter.

Later that year, Schmeling's true character and courage emerged during the Nazi's infamous 'Night of Broken Glass.' They went on a rampage murdering every Jewish man, woman and child they could get their hands on. Schmeling, at the risk of his life, hid two young Jewish boys in his apartment, and later helped them escape from Germany. None of this came out until long after the war.

Schmeling desperately blocks left Louis' left hook but could not stave off defeat, he lasted 124 seconds

Joe now had the world at his feet, and values were slowly changing. Boxing was completely legal and popular, with an Afro American champion who was also popular. In John L. Sullivan's day a large number of title defences entailed more risk than honour. Now it reflected to the champion's glory. Joe cleared the field. He beat some good men, some great ones, plus some who had no business being in the same ring with him. In eleven years he rolled up 25 title defences. Had it not been for the war, he would have rolled up even more. Joe had some hair-raising defences too. On June 28, 1939, he had his hands full with Two Ton Tony Galento. Galento was said to have swilled beer between rounds. He had no respect for anyone. His only comments to the press on meeting Louis for a title fight was, 'I'll moida da bum'. He retracted that statement after the fight. Joe merely referred to him as,' That funny little fat man.' As the fight progressed, both men realised they had been wrong. Joe was certainly no bum, and Galento was by no means funny. He slammed a murderous left hook into Joe's side in the first round, and then shook the boxing world by knocking him down in the second. Then enough was enough. Joe took stock of Galento in the third, and lifted him almost a foot of the canvas to finish it in the fourth. The next year he had another close call with Arturo Godoy from Chile. Godoy's crouching style bothered Joe and the fight went the distance. The decision in Joe's favour did not meet with everyone's approval. Godoy's trainer the legendary Charley Goldman, who was to turn Rocky Marciano into an all-time great, always insisted Rocky was his second heavyweight champion. Joe had Godoy back in the ring with him four months later, and stopped him in eight rounds. The champion also had his hands full with Buddy Baer, Max's 'little 'brother, all six ft. six inches of him. Buddy knocked Joe out of the ring in the first round. Joe got back into the fight but accidentally hit Buddy after the bell ending the sixth round. Buddy refused to come out for the seventh and was disqualified. The following year Joe stopped him in one round.

One of the greatest fighter's Joe ever met was the former world's light heavyweight champion Billy Conn. Billy in fact gave up the light heavyweight title in order to challenge for the heavyweight crown. He almost made it. Joe, by his own admission, always remembered it as his toughest fight. Indeed, it was more a fight Billy lost than one Joe won. Conn's brilliant ring science and footwork took him so far ahead on points, those in the champion's corner told him he could only win by a knock out. Billy's best round, and most of them were good, was the twelfth. It led to his undoing. He battered the champion so badly that he forced him back a few paces. Since Billy was outweighed by 25 lbs, this was no mean feat. Unfortunately for him, it went to his head. He went back to his corner informing his horrified seconds that he was going to knock Louis out. They could not talk him out of it, or more to the point, yell him out of it. Billy felt he was wiser. He even made a statement to Joe as he changed tactics. 'You're having a hell of a fight tonight, Joe,' he said. 'I know it,' replied Joe, then twelve seconds before the round ended, caught the challenger with a powerful left hook and knocked him out.

Billy went on to beat the great middleweight Tony Zale, and went into the army. So did Joe. While in the service he did what he could to defeat racialism by refusing to fight an exhibition before a segregated audience. Joe's much awaited rematch with Billy Conn came five years after their first fight. It drew $1,925,564 dollars at the turn styles, yet it was not a patch on their first encounter. Joe knocked Billy out easily in the eighth round, and then began to think of retirement. First came another title defence. On September 18th 1946 he met a powerful young Italian American Tami Mauriello. Mauriello staggered the champion with a stiff right hand. Joe later admitted that he did not think he could go the distance with him. Instead, he smeared Mauriello's face with his gloves then opened up with an all or nothing combination of blows. Tami went down and out in the first.

Joe hoped his final title defence would be on December 5th 1947, against his onetime sparring partner Jersey Joe Walcott. There was a story that persisted

Joe desperately tries to retain the title against Walcott in the first fight

throughout the fight game that Walcott had once knocked Louis down during a sparring session and as a result he was thrown out of the training camp. .Although this rumour persisted Louis, in turn, claimed to have knocked Walcott down, forcing him to quit the camp. The truth of this may never be known. However, if Jersey Joe *had* quit to fight another day, that day had now arrived, although it almost never happened. The New York Commission thought Jersey Joe's record was so full of losses that the fight ought really to be billed as an exhibition. It took special pleading on the part of the champion for them to sanction it as a title fight.

Walcott , like Jimmy Braddock, was another Cinderella Man. He was also plagued with bad luck and as the father of six children had done his stint working on the docks and been on relief when fights were scarce. Now, thanks to Louis, he had his chance, but showed no gratitude when the fight started. In first round he dumped Joe on the canvas. He out boxed him, and then dumped him again in the fourth. He went on the defensive, counterpunching brilliantly. He had no intention of making the same mistake as Billy Conn. At the end of the fight, everyone was sure the title had finally changed hands. That included Louis. He tried to leave the ring before the decision was announced. He was stopped by a ring official. To the surprise of the crowd and Joe himself, he had retained the title on a split decision.

Joe put off his retirement plans and gave Walcott a much deserved rematch on June 25th 1948. It seemed almost an action replay of their first encounter. Walcott forged his way ahead on points, even dropping the champion. In the eleventh round Joe got some of his old spark back. With a blinding combination of punches he dropped the challenger for the full count. Joe could now retire with dignity, and that was how his admirers wanted him to go out. Louis used a champion's privilege to choose the men to fight to be his successor. He chose Walcott, and a brilliant newcomer to the heavyweight ranks, Ezzard Charles. Both fighters were Afro Americans. Joe's career had showed a weakening of the colour bar. Now the flood gates were open. It seemed strange that Joe himself, in 25 successful title defences, that only two of his challengers were black. That could only mean, like some former champions, that he had not able to choose his challengers. Now the title could be challenged by anyone competent to do so. When all said and done, Joe had much to do with that.

Ezzard Charles keeps the title in his second encounter with Walcott. He lost it in their third

Jersey Joe meets the Cincinnati Cobra

Walcott's prestige was never higher because of his two close fights with Louis. However, on June 22nd 1949 in Chicago, Jersey Joe lost his third attempt at the title to Ezzard Charles. He was then more or less written off, possibly because of his age. Charles a former Golden Gloves champion ,became a great middleweight then one of the great light heavyweights who had outgrown his class. He had defeated some formidable opponents like Anton Christofodis, Teddy Yaros and held Ken Overlin to a draw. He beat Archie Moore no less than three times, their final bout ending in a knockout. As heavyweight champion he started out as a class act. To prove his right to the throne he knocked out Gus Lesnevich, Pat Valentino and Freddie Beshore .

Unfortunately at this time, tax debts, bad investments and an ungrateful government forced the old Brown Bomber to return to the ring. His great charity work was forgotten. Carrying two years ring rust, and without the benefit of any warm up fights, Joe challenged Ezzard for his old title. They met in New York on September 27th 1950. Charles pounded out a one sided 15 round victory over a man he looked up to as his fistic hero. He not only gained universal recognition as champion, but a lot of bad feeling went with it for defeating a boxing legend. Ezzard continued to be a fighting champion, even turning back, once again, the ever persistent Jersey Joe Walcott. Joe had suffered an unexpected set back in losing to a powerful fighter called Rex Layne. Ezzard by passed him to offer Walcott another attempt at the title. He won a clear decision then looked even more impressive in defeating the world's light heavyweight champion, Joey Maxim. There came a demand for yet another Walcott fight. It was to be Joe's fifth attempt. He seemed like a fine wine, growing better with age. On July 18th 1951 in Pittsburgh, Joe metaphorically tore up his birth certificate, and against all odds, flattened Charles in seven rounds to finally take the title. Whether out of gratitude, or public demand, Walcott gave Charles a chance to redeem himself. Their final title fight took place in Philadelphia on June 5th 1952. Joe proved his earlier win over Charles was no fluke. He out boxed the younger man to retain the title on a clear points decision. The basic mantra of professional boxing is, as Muhammad Ali once so beautifully phrased it, 'Money honey.' And if Jersey Joe was seeking a suitable opponent, he suddenly did not have far to look. An elimination contest was held on 27 th July 1952 between Harry Mathews, and an awkward looking Italian American, Rocky Marciano. Mathews was counted out inside two rounds, with his head resting on the bottom rope in his own corner. Walcott accepted Marciano as a challenger. He also went on to make that infamous statement, that if he could not knock out Rocky, who he dismissed as a bum , then his name should be struck off the record books. Fortunately, those who compiled the record books chose to ignore him.

Rocky Marciano: The Brockton Blockbuster
He retained the perfect record

The Brockton Blockbuster.

Marciano, like some great American fighters, had the gift of being a talented baseball player. He was also an excellent tennis player, whose serve was often considered unanswerable. During his army service, while stationed in England, Rocky won a few fights, and was persuaded by his admires to take the game more seriously. Ironically, during his amateur days, he lost a decision to a Joe Louis look alike, Coley Wallace. On turning professional Marciano ploughed his way through everyone they put in front of him. He hoped to be managed by Al Weill, who at first dismissed him. Later, Weill changed his mind and placed him under the guidance of one of the sports great trainers, Charley Goldman. Goldman had been a gifted bantamweight from a bygone era. He moulded Rocky into a formidable fighting machine. Marciano's short arm span, the shortest of all the heavyweight champions, was turned into an asset. His ability to take a punch was comparable to Dempsey, as was his raw punching power. He was rough, crude and tenacious, with the courage of a lion.

Rocky broke into the rankings with a split decision over unbeaten Roland la Starza. In quick succession he blasted out Freddie Beshore in four rounds then, much to his personal regret, finished off the career of Joe Louis. After his loss to Ezzard Charles, Joe had made some considerable success. His best comeback fight had been a knockout victory over the skilful Lee Savold. Savold, for some inexplicable reason was recognised by Britain as the world's champion. Joe did make a claim for that title, but no one took it seriously, least of all Joe himself. He was certainly being considered for another shot at the title. Contrary to popular belief, that the last thing a boxer loses is his punch, this did not quite apply to Joe. He had certainly lost the devastating power in his right hand, but his left hand, as Rocky found out, was as potent as ever. In fact Rocky seemed to have no answer to it. His right eye was badly swollen as Rocky absorbed everything Joe threw at him. He eventually bludgeoned his way to an eighth round stoppage. Joe had administered many a beating in his career. When it came his turn, he went out like a real champion. Rocky went on to beat the elusive Lee Savold, and then stopped Harry Mathews to put himself in line for a title shot.

Walcott set out to prove his statement in Philadelphia on September 23rd 1952. When the first bell rang, Joe's dismissal of Rocky as merely a crude fighter seemed valid. Walcott's body had not aged, nor had he lost his punch. The power that had consistently dropped Joe Louis and blasted out Ezzard Charles was very much in evidence. He went on to be the first man to drop Rocky. Walcott's formidable experience came to bear. He dominated the fight and outclassed the challenger. There was an ugly scene in the seventh round when a substance from Walcott's gloves got in Rocky's eyes. For most of the round he fought almost blind. He survived the round, but the champion needed no unfair advantage. Had Walcott's age been an issue in this fight, he might have tired, but he did not. Other than the first round, when he dropped the challenger, the twelfth round was his best. As the bell sounded for the thirteenth, he had only to stay on his feet to win. Rocky himself was more than aware of that. The round was hardly a minute old when Marciano caught the champion with a right hand from hell. Walcott pitched forward onto the canvas, dead to the world. Rocky was the new heavyweight champion of the world.

Grateful for his chance, Rocky gave Joe a rematch. They squared off in Chicago on May 15th 1953. Rocky needed only 2minutes and 25 seconds to see off the challenger. It was Jersey Joe's last fight. Rocky still had to pay his dues. There was still the business of his split decision with Roland La Starza. They met in New York on September 24th 1953. La Starza, like all challengers for world titles, was in the shape of his life. He out boxed the champion for the first six rounds. Then Rocky, by now warmed up, brought his great strength to bear. He wore the challenger down. In the 11th round the referee had to step in to save the battered La Starza from further punishment. It was said that he received a muttered 'Thanks,' from the challenger

Ex champions never seem to desist when it comes to a chance of reclaiming the title. Ezzard Charles was no exception. He cleared his blemish of by passing Rex Layne, by stopping him in 11rounds. Layne demanded a rematch and defeated Ezzard on points a year later. Charles fought him again to take a 10 round decision. He next defeated Coley Wallace, a top contender, in something of a grudge match. Wallace, as stated, bore a striking resemblance to the young Joe Louis. So much so, that he was asked to play him in a movie on the Bomber's life. Apparently Coley was so taken up with his role that after the movie was finished; he swore he would take revenge on Charles for beating Joe. This was a sore point for Ezzard. He had been unpopular enough Moreover, Joe had been Ezzard's idol, and for that reason he had been reluctant to fight him. Now, in anger, he wanted to confront Wallace in the ring. He did, and finished him off as a top contender. He then showed his old form with a win over highly ranked Bob Satterfield, a fighter known for his ferocious punching power.

Rocky put the title on the line in New York on June 17 1954. If any fighter ever turned the clock back it was Ezzard Charles. His speed was such that the sportswriters had dubbed him the Cincinnati Cobra. His immaculate left jab was said to have been the best since Gene Tunney. He was a master craftsman and he gave Rocky the full benefit of his experience. He was also in the right mental state. Marciano always remembered the fight as the toughest of his career. It was a give and take brawl with the champion's great strength overcoming Charles' speed and brilliance. It was the only time Rocky was taken the full distance in a championship fight. The rematch was not long in coming. Rocky if anything, seemed an improved fighter. The highlight came when Ezzard slashed Rocky's nostril. The referee seemed concerned enough to consider stopping the fight. Rocky begged for one more round and retained the title by flattening Charles in the eighth.

The following May, the active champion used England's Don Cockell as a human punching bag. Cockell showed great courage, but little else. The fight was rough by English standards. There were some cries of foul, but Don was outclassed and went out in nine.

Rocky overpowers the great Archie Moore

Rocky's final fight was against all time great Archie Moore, the world's light heavyweight champion. Rocky's detractors have tried to point out the age of his challengers, including Moore. The obvious reply is to look objectively at their performances rather than their birth certificates. Rocky defended the title against Moore on September 21 1955. Archie first cleared his own division. A year before he had come from behind on points to knock out another all time great, Harold Johnson. He then turned back the challenge of the world's middleweight champion, Carl 'Bobo' Olson. The fight lasted three rounds. He also trounced the huge, highly rated Cuban heavyweight, Nino Valdez. One thing was certain; Archie had not lost his devastating punch. He caught Rocky with a powerful left hook in the second round to become the second man to floor him. Rocky jumped to his feet at the count of four. The referee forgot the rule, and gave Rocky a mandatory eight count. Archie later claimed the referee's action robbed him of the title. Rocky's defenders claimed he got up when he was ready to continue the fight. It became a battle of titans. Archie gave it everything he had, but Rocky's bludgeoning strength was too much for him. In the ninth round Archie collapsed in a heap in his own corner, simply too battered and exhausted to get up.

Rocky then called it a day. He became unique in that he was the one fighter who had never lost a fight. He produced the perfect record with 49 fights with 49 wins. Only six men ever went the distance with him. Tragically, he was killed as a passenger in a light aircraft that crashed through engine trouble. He was truly one of the great names of the sport.

Floyd about to make contact with Ingo's Bingo

Floyd meets Ingo's Bingo

The title was up for grabs again, and filling Rocky's shoes was no easy task. Archie Moore appeared to be the most powerful heavyweight left on the scene. A youngster named Floyd Patterson won an elimination contest for the honour of meeting him. The result was a surprise to some, a disappointment to others. In Chicago on November 30th 1956, Floyd upset the odds and stopped Moore, who carried a tire of fat around his middle, in five one sided rounds. It was debatable as to how much Archie had aged, for he still had some great fights left in him. As for Floyd, he had won a split decision over Tommy 'Hurricane' Jackson, in order to get his chance at a title fight. He paid his dues by stopping Tommy in a one sided title defence in New York. The New York Boxing Commission went on to suspend Tommy's licence. Apparently he had a mysterious manager who knew better, and kept him fighting. After receiving a vicious beating from top liner Eddie Machen, Ring magazine, with some difficulty, tracked down his mysterious manager. It was Tommy's mother. After a blistering article in their pages, she allowed him to quit. Patterson next engaged in a battle that was one for the record books. He defended the title against Pete Rademacher, the Olympic heavyweight champion. It was also Pete's first professional fight. The fight was prophetically one sided, but Rademacher did cover himself with glory. He dropped the champion in the second round. He took a fearful beating after that and was stopped in six. Floyd easily stopped Roy Harris then England's Brian London, but it was felt that he was avoiding his main chief challenger, Eddie Machen. Boxing politics certainly had something to do with this. Floyd's manager, Cus D'Amato was at loggerheads with Jim Norris, who ran the International Boxing Club. Machen was one of Norris' fighter's and consequently D'Amato wanted nothing to do with him. As usual in such cases, Patterson was accused of dodging him.

Despairing of getting a title shot, Machen travelled to Sweden to battle a rated but relatively unknown Ingemar Johannson. Johannson's strongest claim to fame was that he was disqualified in the 1952 Olympic finals against America's Ed Sanders. Ingemar was thrown out for 'not trying'. It took Sweden a long time to forgive him. Yet he possessed dynamite in his right hand. The sportswriters labelled it 'Ingo's Bingo'. He had won the European championship from Franco Cavicchi and turned back Britain's Henry Cooper and Joe Erskine with stunning knock outs. Ingemar continued to stun the boxing world by flattening Eddie Machen in less than a round. Now he was not only Patterson's chief challenger, but he was not affiliated with Jim Norris. Floyd put the title on the line against the Swede on June 26th 1959 in New York. Ingemar was the 4-1 underdog. The fighters got warmed up in the first two rounds, when 'Ingo's Bingo' seemed to develop a mind of its own. It sent the game champion crashing to the deck no less than seven times. The crowd roared, and above it all a hysterical Elizabeth Taylor screamed at referee Ruby Goldstein to stop the slaughter, which he did.

Ingemar set the boxing world talking. Not just by his dynamic performance, but also by his playboy image. Unlike Jim Corbett, Ingemar's image may not have been deceptive. He was known to have kept his lovely girlfriend Birgit Lundgren, with him during training. This caused Marciano to grumble that perhaps he had lived like a monk during his training periods for nothing. Ingemar's next fight caused Rocky to think that his monk like existence had been the right one after all. A year crawled by before the rematch. Patterson had gone into a deep mental depression, and then worked himself up into the shape of his life. As for Ingemar, it was business as usual. His popularity increased as pictures himself and his lovely girl friend graced the sports pages.

Paterson was grimly determined to redeem himself. He was also determined to break the heavyweight jinx. No former titleholder had ever been able to regain it. Great masters such as Corbett, Fitzsimmons, Jefferies, Dempsey, Schmeling, Louis, Walcott and Charles had all tried and failed. Now it was Floyd's turn. In the Polo Grounds in New York on June 22nd 1960, a super fit Patterson dominated the fight. He kept the champion off balance. In the fifth and final round he dropped Johannson, for a nine count. The champion gamely got up when Floyd opened up with everything he had. He hit Ingemar so hard that for a moment only his shoulders were touching the canvas. It was a devastating left hook that finished the job. Marciano stated that that punch had been worthy of Dempsey.

Floyd had succeeded were the immortals had failed. He was to go down in boxing history as the first man to retrieve the undisputed title. Nine months later, they were back in the ring for the rubber match. In Miami Beach on March 13th 1961, both fighters went at it hammer and tongs. Then the fight became sporadic. Floyd finally clinched matters with a sixth round knockout.

Ingemar took the European title back from Dick Richardson. Shortly afterward he retired to become a successful businessman. He married his Birget, and even though they eventually divorced, still managed to live happily ever after. Floyd was not quite so lucky He stopped Tom Mcneeley in four rounds, then defended against a man who outweighed him be 25lbs, outreached him by 13ins, and could hit like Marciano. This was Charles 'Sony' Liston.

Sony Boy

Sony endured a similar lack of popularity as some of his great predecessors. Corbett and Charles had defeated living legends. Dempsey supposedly refused to fight for his country. These however, seemed to be valid reasons for their dislike. With Sony, it was just attitude. His surly uncooperativeness with sportswriters almost guaranteed a bad press. His name was also affiliated with the mob, although there was no reason to assume that his fights were fixed. There was hardly any reason, given his tremendous punching power. Yet it was these alleged connections that kept him away from the

A sight rarely seen in America. A smiling Sony Liston
sits at the back of a London bus with his lovely wife

title for the longest time, as well as a bonafide criminal record. It was Patterson who overrode his manager's advice and forced the issue insisting on giving him a chance. Sony was after all, the chief challenger. As stated, fighters age differently, and Sony may have been passed his best when he challenged Patterson for the crown. If he was, he still had more than enough left to blast Floyd out to take the title. The championship changed hands on September 25th 1962, in Chicago. Liston landed a powerful left hook to end matters in 2min.0 6 seconds of the first round. Sony's lack

Floyd crushed by the overbearing power of Sony Liston

of popularity asserted itself when the new champion arrived at the train station of his new home town Philadelphia. No fans showed up to greet him.

The new champion was said to be one of twenty five children. He grew up to become a juvenile delinquent, and went on to spend time in prison for armed robbery. He was known, amongst other things, to have been a strike breaker, with emphasis on the word break. While serving a prison sentence, the athletic director, Father Stevens encouraged him to take up boxing. Five years passed, when he was good enough to win the 1953 Golden Gloves Tournament. He turned professional shortly after with a knockout studded record. His major wins over the Cuban giant Nino Valdes, Cleveland Williams, who he defeated twice. Eddie Machen took him the full distance

In a one sided bout, then he stopped the chief challenger Zorra Foley inside two rounds. This placed him in line for a title shot. The moralists were against him competing for the championship, and so was Paterson's manager. The fight crowd however, were all for it. And champion Floyd bravely insisted. After his title loss Floyd, much as he had after his defeat by Johansson, went into a depression, then into heavy training for ten months. The rematch was on July 22nd 1963 in Las Vegas. The result was practically the same. The only difference was that Floyd lasted four seconds longer

If Floyd's chances against Sony were considered small, or next to none at all, his next challenger was given even less of a chance. He was a brash young man called Cassius Clay

Cassius Clay before he was Muhammad Ali

The Tangled Times of Muhammad Ali.

Sony's reputation was in tatters after his second title defence, and few had any sympathy for him. It is said that the only certainty in boxing is that there is no certainty. This was borne out by the result of that defence. Liston had sat at the ringside to see his next challenger, a certain Cassius Clay, ten years his junior, fight Doug Jones, the former world's light heavyweight champion. Clay had insulted Jones shamefully, and threatened to knock him out within four rounds. The crowd went wild as Jones had Clay hanging on in the fourth. Clay rallied and won, but Sony felt he had little to worry about from either of them. Most of the sportswriters agreed with him. It is customary to put inverted commas on the word 'experts' who predicted an easy win for Liston, but this is a little unfair. Up to that time, Clay had a good unbeaten record, but it was not particularly outstanding. His first encounter with Britain's Henry Cooper was a near disaster, and led many experts to feel Clay still had much to learn before tangling with the likes of Liston.

Cassius however, had learned his lessons well, and unpredictably blossomed out for the Liston fight. It took place in Miami on February 25th 1964. Clay's plan was to jab and run, tire the champion, and then stretch him beyond the four round limit. The idea being, the longer the fight lasted the better chances for the brash young challenger. The plan was a sound one. An added ingredient was for Clay to psyche Liston before the fight. There was some confusion here. It is possible Clay may have feared Liston's awesome power. Liston was seen to have slapped him to calm the youngster down. The fight doctor, on taking Cassius' blood pressure, claimed it was as high as a man who feared he was about to be shot. Unpredictably, Cassius was calm as entered the ring. As the fight started, Clay's blinding speed upset the champion, but he did enough to keep the fight even. Liston sustained a nasty cut in the third round, but again came back in this round and the next to keep things even on the score cards. In the fifth round Clay found himself in the same situation as Marciano had against Walcott. A substance from Liston's gloves had got into Clay's eyes temporarily blinding him. It took some stern coaxing from his trainer Angelo Dundee, to send him out for the next round. It was a hard fought one that tired the champion, although Fleischer, present at the fight, claimed Sonny was beginning to reach him. As the bell rang for the seventh round all pandemonium broke loose. The fight was suddenly over. Liston was unable to continue due to an injury to his left shoulder and sever eye cuts. Although they were dead even on the scorecards, the brash Cassius Clay was now the undisputed heavyweight champion of the world.

Clay, like so many Afro Americans, then converted to Islam and changed his name to Muhammad Ali. Then, to the disapproval of the W.B.A. he signed for a rematch with Liston. They then took the extreme measure of stripping him of the title. The line of undisputed champions from John L. Sullivan was now broken. With no moral conscience whatsoever, the W.B.A. recognised Ernie Terrell,when he beat Eddie Machen for the what is now known as a Mickey Mouse crown. A fact of which, no one rightly took the slightest notice. Ali's second fight with Liston was even more controversial than he first. It took place on May 25ᵗʰ 1965. It would have taken place before that but Ali sustained a hernia, and the fight had to be postponed. Henry Cooper gave Liston no chance at all on hearing this. He felt the postponement would have been too much for a fighter of Liston's age to get that special edge back. He was probably right, but in the end it made no difference. Ali came out fast with a left right combination to the head. Ali later spoke of another punch that he threw, called the anchor punch. He claimed he learned it from watching the films of Jack Johnson. Unfortunately no one saw it. Liston went down, and lay on his back, presumably unconscious. Perhaps the most memorable thing of the fight was the picture of Ali standing over Liston, snarling at him to get up. The referee Jersey Joe Walcott seemed at a loss at what to do. Ali eventually did rush off to a neutral corner, and Jersey Joe started the count. Liston then got up and continued to fight. At this point Fleischer, sitting at ringside, called out, 'Joe, the fight is over.' It is possible he may also have referred to Liston in a disrespectful manner. But whatever the case, Walcott stopped the fight and hailed Ali as the winner. Many to this day feel the fight was a fix, and that Liston had gone down without being hit, merely to save himself an inevitable beating. Other historians felt that he had been threatened by a Muslim group. Indeed they felt that applied to both title fights. One thing is certain, both these fights left a bad taste at the time. Most of the living former champions were particularly critical. Contemporary experts watching the film of the fight could come up with no evidence that Liston was actually hit. Years later, with more advanced technology, it was seen that Ali did hit him. The so called anchor punch was really an old fashioned uppercut, thrown in the tradition on Fitzsimmons, Johnson, Dempsey and Louis.

After his second loss to Ali, Liston stayed away from the fight game for a year. He was still a powerful fighter, but by no means the fighter he had once been. Sony still chalked up some important wins, although he was knocked out by his former sparring partner Leotis Martin. Sony's manager was negotiating for a fight with George Chuvelo, when he was found dead by his wife in their home. The details to this day remain a mystery. The theory that he died of an overdose did not hold up with the autopsy. Moreover, Sony was said to have had a phobia of needles. The police ruled out foul play, but those close to him had their doubts.

Despite the controversy of the second fight, or perhaps because of it, Ali still had to go onto prove himself to be a great fighter. His showmanship was never in doubt. The seeds of it were more than likely planted in him as a child by watching the wrestler' Gorgeous George' on television. George, whose catchphrase was 'I'm the greatest' deserves a mention here. In reality he was a shy, better than average performer. He had been discharged from the army after the war, and seemed at a loose end. One day, after more than a few beers, George became not so shy, and trusting to his instinct, got his hair permed like a woman at the local hair salon. With a T.V. audience just as horrified and disgusted as those sitting at ringside, George started strutting and mincing around the ring in an effeminate manner, squirting perfume at his opponent, declaring his greatness to the world. A little kid in Louisville Kentucky called Cassius Clay, sitting before the T.V. was drinking all this in. Gorgeous George's method of getting attention was simply by being outrageous, and upsetting. His catch phrase was one the world would get used to hearing long after Gorgeous George was forgotten.

Ali started boxing at the ripe old age of twelve. He maintained a brilliant amateur career. He won six Kentucky Golden Gloves titles, the light heavyweight title at the 1960 Olympics, and the International Golden Gloves at heavyweight. This attracted the attention of a business syndicate who took care of his professional career. Angelo Dundee was given the task of training him. It had been a task Archie Moore had found impossible to undertake. The youngster had simply refused to listen to him. The lessons he had imbibed from Gorgeous George seemed more important to him. The young Cassius was very loquacious, as though daring anyone to close his mouth. He instinctively knew how to attract attention, and developed a genius for manipulating the media. If Gorgeous George could be outrageous, Cassius could go even further.

His climb to the top was not always smooth. He was out boxed by a fighter named Daniels for six one sided rounds. He stopped Daniels on facial cuts in the seventh. His threat to stop Henry Cooper in six rounds almost ended in disaster. Cooper came within a whisker of knocking him out. And after his struggle against Doug Jones, few gave him much of a chance against Liston.

Ali now started to clear up the heavyweight division. Floyd Patterson still sought to regain the crown, and was given his chance on November 22nd 1965. Ever attempting to psyche his opponents, Ali held up a bunch of carrots to the ex champion, with his grinning yes man Bundini standing next to him. The point of this jibe was that Patterson had the courage of a rabbit. Nothing could have been further from the truth. Patterson suffered a one sided beating, badly hurting his back, but stubbornly refusing to quit. The referee Harry Krause stepped in and stopped it in the twelfth. Ali then travelled to Toronto to battle George Chuvalo. George had already battled Ernie Terrill for the Mickey Mouse version of the title, losing in 15 rounds. Now he was challenging Ali for the real thing. After a tough 15 round brawl, Ali retained the title. At this point Ali had trouble with the draught board, which accused of him refusing to go into the army on religious grounds, basically as a conscientious objector. Pending their decision , Ali left the States to defend the title in England and Germany. He fought a rematch with Henry Cooper, who hoped to finish off what he started in their first fight. Ali exploited Cooper's weakness of being easy to cut. Both fights ended in the same manner, with Cooper drenched in blood from facial cuts and the referee stopping he fight. Brian London put up only a token resistance and went out in three rounds. Karl Mildenberger of Germany made a fine early showing. He shook Ali up in the fourth round, landing some good body shots, and driving him across the ring. Ali retaliated and dominated the rest of the fight, finally stopping him in the twelfth. Back in the States Cleveland Williams bravely came forward. Williams had been shot in the stomach, and the doctors who operated on him were forced to leave the bullet embedded in there. Nonetheless, the fight doctors deemed him fit to fight. He lasted three rounds.

Finally came the showdown hardly anyone was waiting for, simply because the result was a foregone conclusion, the battle between Ali and Ernie Terrell, for the 'undisputed championship.' There seemed to have been some bad blood between the two men as Terrill refused to acknowledge Ali's Muslim name. At the end of fifteen

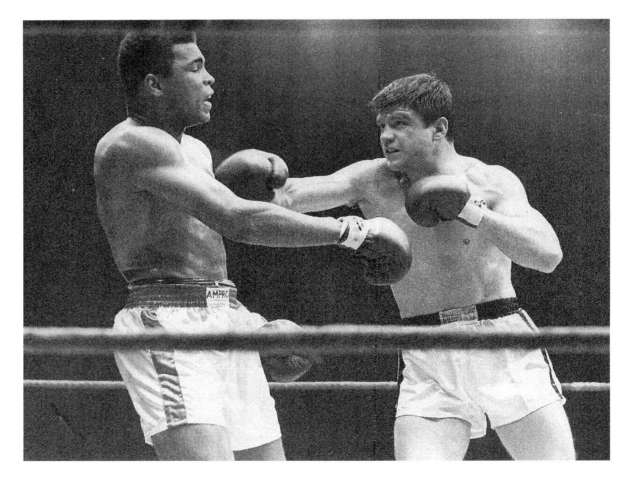

Karl Mildenberger stings Ali into action

one sided rounds, Terrell still refused to acknowledge it, but there was no doubt as to who was the undisputed champion. Ali finally defeated veteran Zora Foley. He came from behind on points to stop the veteran in seven rounds. He then found himself stripped of the title by both the W.B.A. and the New York State Athletic Commission. Their action was based on the findings of a federal grand jury which indicted him on failing to report to the draft board. Ali comments on the Vietnam War were controversial and many Afro Americans who fought in the war, resented them. Later, with hindsight, they started to agree with him. He saw it as a white man's war from which Black America would receive no benefit. His famous statement that 'No Vietcong ever called me a Nigger,' made a lot of people sit up, and it certainly brought a lot of issues into view. His stand was a brave one, from which he risked to lose everything. He was by no means sympathetic to Communism or the Communist ideal. It is doubtful if he and Paul Robeson for example would have seen eye to eye. Yet even Robeson could not have denied the racial barriers Ali knocked down. It was claimed by a Civil Rights brother that Ali had said nothing original, and he would only be remembered for his achievements as a fighter. This is hardly true. Even if his statements were not original, people listened to him, and that was what moved mountains. He was given a five year jail sentence, which he never served, and a fine of $10,000 dollars. The war was unpopular both in America and Europe. Public opinion began to swing in Ali's favour, and after two years he managed to get a licence to fight an exhibition against three low key heavyweights.

Then on October 25th 1970 in Atlanta Georgia, he stopped highly ranked Jerry Quarry in three rounds. In one way it was a disappointing fight. Ali needed to get rid of his accumulated ring rust. Quarry had been an awkward customer, refusing to come at Ali in a straight line. Ali cut him badly in the third round, and over Quarry's protests the fight was stopped. Ali had more luck against tough Oscar Bonavena. He took Ali to the fifteenth round, before his legs gave out for a last round stoppage. It was the sort of fight he needed if he was to get into shape and gain recognition as champion again. Meanwhile Joe Frazier had won a tournament to decide who was champion in Ali's absence. As Ali had not lost the title in the ring, at least the purists still considered him the champion. This was settled on March 8th 1971. For all the awe and adulation Ali was given, Joe Frazier was not exactly one of his fans. He disparaged him, claiming he had only stopped men in their thirties. The tough younger fighters had taken him the distance. Ali in turn, heaped scorn on Frazier. By the time the referee Arthur Mercante told them to touch gloves and come out fighting, there was no love lost between them Ali's immaculate jab went to work on Frazier's face, almost punching it out of shape. Yet Frazier slipped a lot of those jabs. He got inside Ali's guard to pound his body, slowing him down. Frazier pushed himself into a points lead. In the final round he caught Ali with a powerful left hook, knocking him on his back. Frazier won the unanimous decision, gaining final recognition as the undisputed heavyweight champion of the world. For once, if temporarily, the purists and the Mickey Mouse brigade were both satisfied.

Joe Frazier.
His epic battles with Muhammad Ali will never be forgotten

Smoking'Joe.

Joe Frazier, like Muhammad Ali , was another of the great package fighters. He started his career even earlier than Ali, at the age of nine, when he rigged up a home made punching bag. His family moved to Philadelphia from his birthplace in North Carolina. And like many of the old masters, he increased his strength by hard manual labour. In his youth he worked in a slaughterhouse, and was enthusiastic enough to go boxing in the evening.

Joe won the Golden Gloves Tournament two years in a row, then went on to win America's only gold medal in the Tokyo Olympics in 1964. He almost never made it. He was beaten twice by Buster Mathis in the Olympic trials. When Mathis broke a knuckle, Joe was chosen as a substitute.

Some entrepreneur businessmen called Cloverleaf Inc. on the lookout for Olympic boxing gold medallists, grabbed him up and launched his professional career. He chalked up ten knockouts in a row before taking on top liner Oscar Bonavena. Joe picked himself of the deck twice in the second round before pounding out a ten round decision. He then scored an important win over George Chuvalo. He became the first man to stop George in his fifteen year career. Finally Joe cleaned the slate by stopping his old rival Buster Mathis him in 11rounds. This was a year after Ali was stripped of the title; Frazier's victory at least gave him the New York version of the title. Joe had beaten everybody around. Two years later with Ali still not yet back in the picture, Frazier won 'universal' recognition as overall champion by stopping Jimmy Ellis in four rounds. Joe then looked formidable in defending the title against the great world's light heavyweight champion Bob Foster. He needed less than two rounds to do it. By this time Ali was back, and the showdown was inevitable. Joe then proved his right to the throne in a gruelling 15 round fight. For the purists Frazier won the title from the defending champion, because Ali had not lost it in the ring.

Joe took on two easy defences before taking on the much feared newcomer, George Foreman. Frazier blasted out Terry Daniels, a 15-1 underdog in four rounds, then destroyed Ron Stander, a 20-1 underdog in five rounds. The odds were much better for George. He was a 3-1 underdog. The fight was held in Kingston Jamaica on January 22nd, 1973.

Against all expectations, the fight was very one sided. Frazier had no answer to Foreman's dynamic punching power. George seemed to be a bigger version of Sony Liston. He possessed the same overbearing punch, but he was much younger. Moreover, given Frazier's nonstop attacking style, Foreman did not have to go looking for him. He dropped the champion three times in the first round. In the second and final round George literally lifted Frazier a foot off the ground. He gamely climbed off the canvas three more times before referee Arthur Mercante wisely put a stop to it.

George Foreman
The greatest granddad of them all

Big George

George Foreman was the new heavyweight champion of the world other than being a gold medallist. Foreman resembled Sony Liston in that he was another 'bad boy' who was saved by boxing. He won the National A.A.U. heavyweight championship that earned him a place on the Olympic team in Mexico. On turning professional he was guided towards the title, and he certainly earned his chance. He won thirty seven straight fights. Thirty four of them never lasted the distance. For all that, when he signed to fight Frazier for the title, as seen, the betting odds were strongly against him. As defending champion he stretched his knock out record to thirty six. He looked formidable in stopping challenger Joe Roman in less than a round. He then gained a reputation for terror, in stopping his next challenger Ken Norton, in only two rounds. Muhammad Ali, by his own admission claimed he had not gone back very far, when he met Norton who took a 12 round split decision over him. Norton even had the temerity to break Ali's jaw. The rematch ended in another split decision, with Ali the winner, but there was very little between them. Norton however, never gave Foreman the slightest bit of trouble. In truth it was a one sided walkover, and Norton admitted the last thing he wanted was a rematch. Now Ali loomed up as George's number one challenger. And admittedly, he worked hard to achieve it. Like all his great and not so great predecessors, he was obsessed with getting the title back.

Most of the sportswriters did not just think Ali had his work cut out for him, they feared for him. After redeeming himself with Norton, Ali met his old adversary Joe Frazier, for the honour of taking on Foreman. Their fight was almost a carbon copy of their first bout. Yet it was a twelve rounder, and Ali took a close points decision. It was a controversial fight, for all that. Frazier accused Ali of showboating. Namely, landing ineffectual punches that merely looked good to catch the judge's eye, while he felt he had landed the more effective blows. Whatever the case and many sports writers agreed with Frazier, Ali's title challenge was set for Zaire on October 3rd 1974.

Once in Africa, the Ali magic started to work. He called the fight 'The Rumble in the Jungle' and played on his immense popularity, endearing himself to the local populace. Within a short time, George hardly had a friend in the place. Indeed, their lack of knowledge was such that many thought Ali was the champion and George was the challenger. When the fight eventually got under way, the crowd cried out almost to a man, 'Ali, Bomba-ya,' which in plain English simply meant,' Ali, kill him.' It was also revealed that before the fight, Ali bribed the men who put up the ring to keep the ropes slack. Had they not been so loose, Ali could not have fought as he had. Then came a postponement as George received an eye cut during a sparring session Ali made good use of the time drumming up more support. Rightly or wrongly, he felt this was having an effect on the champion. Ali hogged the spotlight even more when he introduced a beautiful young girl as his wife. The T.V. cameras and millions of on lookers worldwide were captivated and moved by her looks. So was Ali's wife back in the States. She caught the next available flight out to Kinshasa, and presumably George Foreman became the least of his worries.

Finally, before a crowd of 62,000 people, they squared off. Ali stayed away from Foreman's devastating power although he briefly got caught in the first round. George somehow let him off the hook. He also showed his own blinding speed had not diminished. He was now thirty two years old, which can be a good age for a heavyweight. Ali moved away, constantly talking to the champion, trying to upset and psyche him. As the fight wore on, he began to lie back on the loosened ropes, for a manoeuvre he coined the 'Rope-a-Dope.' Foreman fell for it. He pounded Ali as best he could, but could not get his leverage. Ali, for most part, swayed and rode the punches. It was not the kind of fight George had trained for. He blindly put his faith in his overwhelming power, which was waning as the fight progressed. Some sports writers sitting at ringside began to suspect that the title might change hands. By the eighth round the champion was becoming arm weary, while Ali was relatively fresh. Suddenly, he came off the ropes to punch squarely on Foreman's jaw. Yet many at ringside thought George was felled more by exhaustion than Ali's blows. Back in his dressing room Ali gave all the credit to Allah, reminding sportswriters that he could not hit. No one knew what to say. But whether it was from divine intervention or not, Ali was once again the undisputed heavyweight champion of the world.

Now it was George's turn to wander in the ex champions wilderness. He claimed to have realised his mistakes. He even accused Ali of cheating him out of the title, but in reality, it seemed neither fighter was keen on a rematch. Nevertheless, George went on a comeback trail. He destroyed Frazier again, but this time it took him six rounds. He then took on Jimmy Young. Young was a good craftsman who did a craftsman like job on him. Ali had removed the fear many fighters held of George and the ex champion found he was out boxed, knocked down, and finally taken to hospital in a state of exhaustion. He dropped out of the game for ten years, and then made what had to be the greatest comeback of them all .

Ali now set out to try and beat Joe Louis record of title defences. He met some good men, and padded his record with men who were not so good. Then on October 1st 1975 in Manila Ali fought Joe Frazier for the third and last time. There was still no love lost between the two men. Frazier still took Ali's jibes seriously, and due to Muhammad's popularity, his kids were being bullied at school. Moreover Frazier smarted over the decision of their last fight, which he considered he had won. Ali in turn, dismissed Frazier as a fighter, feeling he could take anything Joe could throw at him. If any two men earned each other's respect the hard way, it was in this fight. Ali dubbed it 'The thrilla in Manila', and he certainly got that right. From the first bell, the two men set out to pummel each other severely. First Ali forged ahead, then Frazier. Ali's vaunted jab again began to change the shape of Frazier's face. Frazier broke through and pounded Ali's body. At times the champion lay on the ropes, as he had done with Foreman. This time the roped were not slack and Ali absorbed a fearful beating. By the tenth round, they were even on the score cards in a fight it must have been difficult to score. For Frazier, he seemed to be putting his life on the line. Gradually they fought each other to a standstill. By the end of the fourteenth round, Ali admitted he was ready to quit. Frazier could hardly see, and was barely able to stand. Over his protests, Joe's manager Eddie Futch stopped the fight. It was a long time before he spoke to him again. After the fight, Ali was generous in his praise, and perhaps the bad feeling between them mellowed.

Ali continued to be a fighting champion. Yet his victories over Jimmy Young and Ken Norton raised some questioning eyebrows. After the Young fight, one sportswriter suggested that perhaps the only way a champion could lose his title was by a knock out. Ali was clearly feeling the strain. Alfredo Evangelista and Ernie Shavers both went the distance with him in title fights. Then he came up with an idea that only his most devoted admirers could accept. He would generously give an unknown a chance at the title, In this case the unknown was a gifted, but not very experienced Leon Spinks, the older brother of Michael, a future world light heavyweight , then heavyweight champion. Leon had a brilliant amateur record, winning the light heavyweight gold medal at the1976 Olympics. He had beaten some good professionals but hardly warranted a shot at the title. Nevertheless, he got one.

On February 15th 1978, with only seven professional fights under his belt, Leon won a unanimous decision and took the crown. Leon, given his lack of experience, felt it safe to give the waning Ali a rematch. In the real world the W.B.A. demanded that Leon defend the title against Ken Norton. Such a match would have been suicide. Leon went ahead and defended against Ali. The W.B.C. stripped him of the title. The W.B.A. still recognised him, and it was this version that Ali regained by beating the youngster on September15 1978 in New Orleans. It was then that Ali wisely, if temporarily, retired. From the purist's point of view, the undisputed championship was up for grabs again.

Larry Holmes
He fought and beat most of the good men of his day

Larry Holmes

Since the W.B.C. had stripped Leon Spins of the title, they did not recognise Muhammad Ali's claim. Instead they declared Ken Norton as the new champion on the strength of his split decision win over Jimmy Young. This claim was not taken too seriously. But when Norton lost to Larry Holmes for the W.B.C. version of the title, Holmes was given universal recognition, basically because he was the best around. A former truck driver, Holmes sharpened his skills as a sparring partner for Muhammad Ali. When he beat Earnie Shavers, allegedly one of the most dangerous punchers in the history of the game, he was given a chance at Ken Norton for the W.B.C. crown. He proved to be a fighting champion and strengthened his claim with stoppage wins over an aging Muhammad Ali and later Leon Spinks. All the leading contenders were beaten by him. His most famous defence was against a potential all time great Gerry Cooney. It was a potential that was never realised. Cooney had scored knockouts over such major fighters as Jimmy Young and Ron Lyle. He then blasted out Ken Norton in 54 seconds. Unfortunately, his brains trust rushed him into a title fight with Holmes before he was ready for it. Inexplicably, Cooney, who needed more experience before battling a fighter of Holmes calibre, accumulated eleven months ring rust. For some reason, as the contract was signed, Cooney was obliged to ask Holmes permission for another a warm up fight. Holms refused. On June 11th 1982 in Las Vegas, Cooney fought a game fight but succumbed in the 13th round, on a disqualification.

After defending the title against Fran Scott, Holmes gave up his W.B.C. title for the newly formed I.B.F. For those who still cared about the significance of one universally accepted champion, this was a heavy blow for the purists. Yet the majority of fans and sportswriters still considered Larry the champion, namely on the grounds that no fighter had taken the title away from him. This changed on September 21st 1985 in Las Vegas. Leon Spinks younger brother Michael, the world's light heavyweight champion redeemed the family honour by out pointing Larry in 15 close rounds. This was a bitter blow for Larry as he had hoped to equal, then surpass Marciano's record of 49 unbeaten fights.

Now Holmes joined his predecessors in trying to reclaim the championship. Spinks offered him that chance on April 19th 1986. They fought again in Las Vegas and he result was the same. Spinks retained the title over 15 close rounds.

Leon Spinks
He may have been given his chance too soon

The Spinks Brothers

Michael came from one of the most talented boxing families in the history of the game. The Spinks brothers were unique in boxing as a fighting family. Their names will be linked to the great Gibbons brothers, the Zivic family, and later the Klitschko brothers. Both the Spinks brothers showed their pedigree by winning gold medals at middle and light heavyweight at the 1976 Olympics, and both were considered by boxing purists to have held the undisputed heavyweight championship of the world. Leon was the less successful of the two. Many felt Muhammad Ali gave Leon his chance before he was ready. This may have been borne out by his crushing one round defeat at the hands of Gerrie Coetzee after his title loss to Ali. He finished his career with 27 losses against his name. Possibly with the reputation of an ex champion with only nine fights under his belt, he was unable to develop, being forced to fight far more experienced fighters. He nonetheless had the satisfaction of seeing his son Cory become a world welter and light middleweight champion.

Michael was the more proficient fighter. He became the W.B.A. world's light heavyweight titleholder, and then went on to claim the undisputed heavyweight crown with his victory over Larry Holmes. He defended the title against Steffen Tangstad, stopping him in four rounds. Then, after a lapse of five years, Gerry Cooney decided he wanted to fight again, preferably for the title. It loomed up as a big money fight, and Michael was happy to oblige him. Unfortunately, the I.B.F. didn't think much of the idea and a pencil happy bureaucrat put a line through Michael's name, and stripped him of the title. It was easy. They wanted him to defend the title against Tony Tucker, as well he might after the Cooney fight, but why wait?

Other than fighting gamely, Cooney could not shake off five years ring rust and went out in five rounds. Meanwhile another all time great came on the scene, and he was no less controversial as his most controversial predecessors.

Iron Man Mike Tyson
The Baddest Man on the Planet

Iron Mike and more entanglements.

Mike Tyson was another of the 'bad boy's' of boxing and possibly the greatest. Indeed, he took a pride in being the 'baddest man on the planet.' He was of the same calibre as Ali, Marciano and Louis. As a troubled teenager, in and out of detention centres, he was sent to the Tryon School for boys. He was certainly a youth at war with the world, who took a delight in beating up other kids and vulnerable adults. His potential as a boxer was noticed by the instructor who taught him the basics of the game. He was so impressed with the youth's progress he referred him to Floyd Paterson's old manager and trainer Cus D' Amato. Tyson was released to the old man's care. D'Amato nurtured him, and turned him loose on the heavyweight division in 1985. In his first 27 fights, he stopped 25 of them, 15 in the first round. He was incorporated in a title unification series, when on November 22nd 1986, he destroyed Trevor Berbick inside two rounds. As such he laid a claim to be the youngest man to at least a version of the heavyweight title. Spinks still had the strongest claim and they certainly were heading on a collision course. Some sports writers, to their credit traced a line from John L. Sullivan directly to Spinks. They saw other pretenders to the crown as holding the afore mentioned Mickey Mouse titles.

Tyson sought to unify the title and no one was better suited to do so. James 'Bone Crusher' Smith came next. On March 7th 1987 Mike took Smith's W.B.A. version of the title. Smith seemed more intent on lasting the distance, which he did. Five months later 'Iron Mike pounded out another 12 round points decision over Tony Tucker for I.B.F. title and allegedly, the undisputed championship. Yet Michael Spinks was still undefeated. The confusion was such that many contemporary historians, even to this day, do not consider Tyson's devastating 91 second knockout of Spinks as a title fight. Yet for the purists, this was the fight that gave Mike the title. Their logic was simple. Holmes was the champion. He was beaten by Spinks, who in turn was beaten by Tyson. They see it as simply as that.

At this point the heavyweight scene had never seemed healthier. Tyson was not just an all time great, which is what the fight game needed, but he was also universally accepted as champion. Moreover, there was no one on the fistic horizon capable of beating him; except himself. Tyson next beat England's Frank Bruno in five rounds. Then a newly formed boxing body calling itself the W.B.O. decided to bang another nail in the coffin of the fight game, by announcing they would recognise the winner of the bout between Francesco Damiani and Johnny Du Plooy. According to them Tyson's efforts had been meaningless. According to the fans, Tyson would have beaten Damiani and Du Plooy on the same night. In essence, they were releasing more Mickey Mouse titles. Both 'contenders' wisely avoided Tyson. Mike went on to flatten Carl Williams inside a round in another bona fide title defence.

Yet at a time when the fight game needed him the most, some began to worry about Mike's life style. Floyd Patterson shuddered at the drink he concocted for himself, and then things started to fall apart. D'Amato and his benefactor Jacobs had died. Don King then ousted his other benefactor Cayton. His marriage to the actress Robin Givens ended in a painful divorce, and he split with his old time trainer Kevin Rooney .Then in Tokyo on February 11ᵗʰ 1990 he defended the title against James 'Buster' Douglas. Mike was certainly not in the mental or physical shape he should have been. The challenger on the other hand, at least for once in his career, was in the shape of his life. 'Buster' dominated most of the fight. Mike rallied in the eighth round to put Douglas down. There was talk of a long count. The referee was slow in starting it. Some thought Douglas had been on the deck for as long as 13 seconds. Don King protested, but no official complaints were made. Tyson had shot his bolt. Douglas came back to knock out Iron Mike in the tenth round. A new star was born, even if it quickly fizzed out. In fact, to the disappointment of most fight fans, they both fizzed out. Rather than fight a rematch, Tyson chalked up four wins in a row, and spent the next three years in prison on an alleged rape charge. He was never again the same fighter. The new champion was apparently addicted to junk food, and lost the title to Evander Holyfield in a pathetic performance that lasted less than three rounds. Tyson's only comments were, 'I lost the title to a bum.'

Evander Holyfield, ex champs and Mickey Mouse Inc.

After George Foreman's defeat by Jimmy Young, the ex champion looked for excuses, then he stopped fooling himself. Despite his tremendous punching power, George had not really learned his ring craft. He decided to quit. Like Bob Fitzsimmons, Tommy Burns and Henry Armstrong, George became a preacher.

Yet he still felt he had unfinished business. The lure of the ring made him try just one more time, and it was a very long time. Ten years elapsed for what turned out to be the greatest comeback of them all. George had the strength of character to put his losses behind him and seek the title again. He was clearly not the fighter of his youth, but he had yet to lose his punch. Moreover, his comeback trail was also a learning process.

He managed to stop another comeback fighter, Gerry Cooney. George lost the first round, but he caught Gerry in the second round with his anywhere punch. It was an impressive victory. He was defeated by defending champion Evander Holyfield.. Evander in turn, was defeated by Michael Moorer the former world's W.B.O light heavyweight champion, and the first southpaw to gain that title. Michael looked for a money match by defending against Foreman. It looked like a routine defence until the tenth round, when George made fight history by flattening the champion for the full count. Twenty years had passed since he had lost the title to Muhammad Ali. George suddenly became everyone's favourite granddad. True to form, the W.B.A. stripped him of its version of the title and he eventually relinquished his I.B.F. recognition. After some dubious showings he retired to make a fortune selling a grill that carried his name.

Evander Holyfield started out as a light heavyweight bronze medallist in the 1984 Olympics. He won the W.B.A world cruiserweight title against Carlos De Leon, then became the undisputed heavyweight champion by stopping James 'Buster 'Douglas in three rounds in Las Vegas on October 25th 1990. He went on to turn back ex champion George Forman , stopped Bert Cooper, then another ex champ, Larry Holmes.On November14th 1992 he was defeated by Riddick Bowe.

Riddick relinquished the W.B.C. recognition rather than fight England's Lennox Lewis, the fighter who had stopped him in the 1988 Olympics. However, Bowe still retained recognition from the W.B.A. and I.B.F. and consequently turned back Michael

Dokes and Jesse Ferguson . Holyfield cleared things up by beating Riddick. Then Moorer relieved him of the title to lose it, as stated, to George Foreman. As Georges claim evaporated the confusion grew greater, and Mickey Mouse Inc was enjoying the time of its life.

Mike Tyson, now released from prison, was eager to re-establish himself. How much he had lost in his three years in prison remained to be seen. Barry McGuigan prophetically said that Mike might win some of the lesser titles, but he doubted if he would do well against the major title holders. Iron Mike did grab one title After many attempts England's Frank Bruno edged out Oliver McCall to take the W.B.C. version of the title. Frank had failed bravely against Tim Witherspoon, Mike Tyson and Lennox Lewis in title bouts. Now, their roles were reversed, Tyson challenged him for W.B.C. recognition. Iron Mike had stopped Frank in Las Vegas in 1989 in five rounds. Now, seven years later, they were to meet again. Las Vegas was again the venue, and Iron Mike did the job in only three rounds, .Yet clearly they were both past their best. Mike picked up another title, the W.B.A. by stopping Bruce Seldon in one round. Bruce swore on a stack of bibles that he never went down without being hit, and it took a while for the fight authorities to believe him, such was the terrify reputation of Iron Mike. The moment of truth came two months later when he took on Evander Holyfield with the W.B.A. version at stake. The Purists considered this fight the 'real' one for the undisputed championship. It proved once and for all however, that Tyson was a long way from the great fighter he had once been. Against a fighter of Holyfield's calibre he showed little of his former self. In the eleventh round the referee stepped in and raised Evander's hand in victory. Because of Tyson's former greatness and current drawing power, they were back in the ring seven months later. It never should have happened. Realising he had no chance of winning, Mike left his gum shield in his corner, and viciously bit off a chunk of Holyfield's ear. The referee was reluctant to disqualify him. So Mike bit off a chunk of Evander's other ear in the following round. With little choice , the referee finally disqualified him. Mike was not banned for life, although it may have been kinder to him to have done so. Holyfield contemplated suing him, but changed his mind. For all the protests in the press, Mike's licence was not revoked. In reality, he was exploited for his once formidable reputation, and for once other fighters were not reluctant to fight him. They may have been seriously wary of being bitten, but given the dividends, they were prepared to take the chance. The multiple boxing associations refrained from making comment. Mike was allowed to battle on.

Lennox Lewis
The second undisputed heavyweight champion to be born on English soil

Britain's pride, Lennox Lewis

Lennox Lewis was something of a late developer, but he was most popular in Britain as being the second heavyweight champion to have been born on British soil. Born in London, he was taken to Canada as a child where he took up boxing. He had a brilliant amateur record and represented Canada in the 1988 Olympics. It was there that he stopped Riddick Bowe in two rounds to win the super heavyweight gold medal.

Lennox returned to England, turned professional and won the British, Commonwealth and European titles. This steady progress made him a world class performer. He was awarded the W.B.C. version of the title when Riddick Bowe the title holder, reneged on a promise to defend against him. Lennox out pointed Tony Tucker, then stopped Frank Bruno and Phil Jackson to retain his title. Some questions were raised about his ability when Oliver McCall stopped him inside two rounds. Three years later Lennox took his revenge in what many felt was a none event. McCall suffered from some kind of emotional breakdown and was led weeping from the ring. It went down in the record books as a fifth round stoppage for Lennox. Lewis gained more credibility when he stopped Andrew Golota in one round. What may have inspired Lennox was that Golota had in turn been inspired by Tyson biting chunks out of Holyfield's ears. He threatened to do the same to Lennox.

Lennox went on to defend against Shannon Briggs and Zeljko Mavrovic, but the real showdown was to be against Evander Holyfield. Evander held the strongest claim to the title, especially with his two wins over Tyson. In New York, on May 13th 1999, Lennox and Evander boxed to a twelve round draw. It was considered one of the worst decisions in years. So much so, that an official investigation was held on the corruption of boxing. The decision went down in the record books, but a rematch was ordered six months later. This time there were no slip ups. Lennox pounded out a unanimous decision for universal recognition as the undisputed heavyweight champion .

Lennox stopped David Grant and Frans Botha in two rounds apiece then out pointed David Tua to retain the title. Unexpectedly Lennox ran into trouble against Haseem Rahman and was flattened in five rounds. The trouble was blamed on Lennox taking part in the 'Oceans Eleven' movie. It was claimed to have taken him out of his stride. He also took Rahman too lightly. Seven months later Lennox regained the title via a four round knock out.

The mayhem started when a Lewis Tyson fight was arranged. Tyson was hardly in physical or mental shape for such a fight, but the dollars were calling. Apparently they were not calling loud enough. Nevada refused to give 'Iron Mike' a licence to box, so that ruled out Las Vegas. Memphis was not so particular. Mike had not changed. At a pre fight conference he completely lost it and bit Lennox on the leg. The fight went through anyway. Tyson showed a glimmer of his former self by taking the first round. After that it was all Lewis, who ended matters in the eighth round. Lennox next made a poor showing against Vitali Klitschko. Trailing on points, he cut the challengers eye and the referee stopped the bout. Vitali was keen on a rematch but Lennox called it a day. Tyson boxed on for two more years, losing to men who could not have carried his bucket when he was in his prime. He was eventually declared bankrupt.

The Brothers Klitschko

The Klitschko brothers were the sons of a Soviet air force colonel, and consequently brought up in a middle class background. Like most children of military personnel, they were moved around from place to place. They finally settled in Kiev were Vitali, the elder brother, developed into a good kick boxer. He was good enough to enter for the 1996 Olympics. He was ruled out when a doctor massaged a leg injury that contained a banned substance. He then made the decision to become a professional fighter.

Vitaly won the W.B.O. version of the heavyweight title by stopping Herbie Hide inside two rounds in 1999. However, while leading on points over Chris Byrd, he quit due to a shoulder injury. Consequently, the American T.V. circuit lost interest in him. He came back to prominence with his impressive battle against Lennox Lewis.

Chris Byrd did not retain the W.B.O.title for long. He lost it to Vitaly's younger brother Wladimir, through a twelve round points decision. Now both brothers were active headliners.Wladimir was considered the more gifted of the two brothers. At six and a half feet, he carries a powerful punch in both hands and possesses a good ring brain. He won a gold medal at the 1996 Olympics and turned pro alongside his brother under the same management. He avenged his brother's defeat by outclassing Byrd over twelve rounds. Indeed, the brothers have spent some time avenging each other. Corrie Sanders took Wladimir's W.B.O. title on March 8th 2003. Vitali stopped Sanders a year later for the W.B.C. title. He stopped Danny Williams then announced his retirement. Wladimir went on to stop Chris Byrd in seven rounds to take the I.B.F. title on April 22nd 2006. Wladimir, to date holds he strongest claim in that, Mickey Mouse notwithstanding, a line, admittedly a shaky one, can be reasonably traced all the way back to the Boston Strong Boy.

What we have is admittedly a tangled web that is robbing the game of all respect and credibility. Don King's unifying tournament was a step forward, but hardly offered an answer, when any accepted champion can be stripped of the title without a moments notice. One possible answer might be for these divergent boxing bodies to amalgamate into one body, and recognise one champion at each given weight. And once such a body came into being, it should be made illegal for anyone else to set up a similar organisation. With money the overall object, this could be an impossible demand, but it is not an unreasonable one. Apart from Nat Fleischer, who the cynics laughed at when he wanted to complain to the president of the United States, no other real protest has ever been made. Fleischer saw clearly what was going to happen, and those that care about the game can only hope that while his worst fears have come into being, they might not be irreversible.

It may seem unfair that many fighters who have claimed a version of the title have not been mentioned. However, we have tried to keep as close as possible to the line that was intact before stripping a champion of his title became an unopposed pastime.

In bygone days a champion could only lose his title in the place where he won it, in the ring. One champion at each given weight might at least put some credibility and respect back into the sport. It might even give it back its lost popularity to the general sports lover.

A note of thanks to Harold Alderman, for offering helpful notes. To Laura Haston and Paul for their time and patience and to Larry Braysher for the use of his photographs, some of which are very rare.

Biographical note:

The author was born in London and served as a merchant seaman at sixteen He joined the Canadian Army at eighteen and was considered a good prospect on the fight cards. Faulty eyesight stopped any ambitions he might have had in the fight game. He lived in Amsterdam and Paris before returning to England where he took his degree in Fine Arts at St. Martin's School of Art in London. He has written books for young adults and articles on boxing, the latest of which was published in the Boxing Yearbook, 2010.